Stephen Castles

# MIGRANT WORKERS
# AND THE TRANSFORMATION
# OF WESTERN SOCIETIES

Cornell Studies in International Affairs

Western Societies Papers

Stephen Castles is the director of the Centre for Multicultural Studies at the University of Wallongong, Australia. He is the author of many articles and books including *Here for Good Western: Europe's New Ethnic Minorities* (Pluto) and co-authored *Immigrant Workers and Class Structure in Western Europe* (Oxford) with Godulka Kosack, and *The Education of the Future* (Pluto) with Wiebke Wustenberg.

# MIGRANT WORKERS AND THE TRANSFORMATION OF WESTERN SOCIETIES

Stephen Castles

Western Societies Program
Occasional Paper No. 22
Center for International Studies
Cornell University
1989

# Contents

# Introduction

Since 1945 nearly all the advanced industrial countries have experienced mass migrations, which have had a lasting and irreversible impact on our societies. Millions of people in search of work and a better livelihood, and sometimes of political freedom and protection from persecution as well, have flooded into Western Europe, North America, and Australia. They have come from Southern Europe, Latin America, Asia and Africa. In most cases, the first people to migrate have been workers—some intending to stay only for a few years, others with permanent settlement in mind. Everywhere these migrant workers have been followed by family members, and a large proportion have settled for good. The result has been the unplanned development of ethnic and racial minorities throughout the developed world. The situation of these minorities varies too widely to be summed up in a few words: in some countries, certain ethnic groups suffer marked social disadvantage and racism, and serious conflicts have arisen. In other cases, policies of multiculturalism and social justice have been introduced to safeguard the rights of minorities. But everywhere the trend towards ethnic diversity is challenging prevailing ideas on national identity and culture. Labor migration has become a major force for social and political transformation in the contemporary world.

This development needs to be placed in its socio-economic and historical context. The period since the Second World War has been marked by growing integration of the international economy. Markets for capital, raw materials and industrial products have become global in scope, and control of the world economy is increasingly concentrated within huge transnational corporations. The international mobility of labor is a central aspect of this process of this development.

Nor is international migration a new phenomenon: it is as old as capitalism. Its earliest forms were movements of European settlers to the New World at the beginning of the colonial era, together with forced recruitment of black slave labor for the plantations. As industrialization started in the 18th and 19th centuries, the new mill towns pulled in rural workers from the surrounding countryside. When these were no longer sufficient to satisfy the factories' ravenous appetite for labor power, currents of international migration got under way: from Ireland to England and Scotland; from Poland to the Ruhr; from Italy to France and Switzerland; and from all parts of Europe to the North America and other parts of the New World. These "great migrations" reached a peak in the period 1870-1914, and then declined during the period of world economic stagnation and crisis which lasted until 1945.

What was new about the post-1945 migrations was their sheer volume, their rapid growth, their general nature embracing nearly all advanced countries, and the frequent role of government in recruitment and control of workers. In many cases attempts were made to recruit

1

temporary workers—the "Gastarbeiter" in Germany, the "braceros" in the USA—who were intended to not settle or bring in dependents. In other cases, permanent migration was envisaged, but selection, admission and utilization of workers was still based on economic criteria.

For most countries (those of Western Europe and Australia) there were two distinct periods of migration policy: from 1945 to about 1974, primary migration (i.e. of workers) was encouraged as a solution to labor shortages during a period of rapid expansion. Family reunification and settlement occurred, but the primary concern was an economic one. From the mid-1970s, when the "oil crisis" heralded the period of economic crisis and restructuring, primary migration was curtailed—indeed it was almost completely stopped in most Western European countries (except for people moving within regional economic blocs like the European Community or the Nordic Labor Market. In this second period, most migration has been family reunification, and processes of settlement have been predominant. The emphasis in academic and political discourse has shifted from the economy to issues of social conflict, public order and cultural change.)

The largest immigration country since 1945 (as before 1914) has been the USA. Here the two periods are somewhat different: intakes were between 100,000 and 200,000 per year from 1945 to 1965. Then the new Immigration Act, which emphasized family reunion as a ground for entry, led to an upsurge in entries. By the 1980s up to 600,000 people were coming in as legal permanent immigrants each year. The number of illegal entrants can only be guessed at, but certainly run into the millions for the period as a whole.

As the migrations developed, people tended to come from areas more distant in cultural and ethnic terms: initial postwar migrants to Western Europe were from Ireland, Finland and Southern Europe; later entrants came from Turkey, North Africa, West Africa, Asian and the Caribbean. Australia at first sought new blood in Northern and Eastern Europe; later migrants came from Southern Europe, then from Turkey and the Lebanon, later from South East Asia and the Indian sub-continent. The USA and Canada received mainly European migrants in the immediate postwar years, but since the mid-1960s most have come from Latin America and Asia.

The eurocentric societies which dominated the world in the 19th and early 20th centuries thus find themselves doubly questioned: from without, by the rise of new industrial powers in Asia, Latin America and the Arab world; and from within, by a new ethnic and racial diversity. The postwar migrations have changed the world, but we have yet to come to terms with the transformation and its implications for the future of our societies and for international relations.

The essays in this collection are the product of twenty years of observation of the developing international migrations. I started working on this theme at Sussex University in 1968 together with Godula Kosack. The main product of that cooperation was the book *Immigrant Workers and Class Structure in Western Europe* (London, Oxford University Press, 1973 and 1985), one of the first international comparative works on the topic in the English language. After some years working mainly on education, I returned to the area in the early 1980s and my "second look" after the end of the period of labor recruitment was published as *Here for Good—Western Europe's New Ethnic Minorities* (London, Pluto Press, 1984). I now continue to work on migration, settlement and ethnic relations in Australia, as Director of the Centre for Multicultural Studies at the University of Wollongong.

The collection is the result of a period as Visiting Scholar at the Western Societies Program of Cornell University in the Spring Semester of 1988. It owes much to the support of John Weiss and John Oakley of the WSP. We realized that most of my works on international migration were relatively inaccessible to American readers, and it was decided to bring out a collection which might be useful to US students in this field. The aim was not to present a current overview, but rather to make available older and newer analyses, which will help people to follow not only the development of the phenomenon, but also the emergence of one particular way of looking at it. No attempt has been made to change or update the papers in any way. They reflect different epochs in the study of postwar labor migration. However a few words on the context of the various articles seem appropriate.

"Bidonville—A French Word for Hell," was written in 1969 as a journalistic piece, after Godula and I had visited the shanty-towns surrounding Paris. At that time one merely had to look for large building-sites; one could be sure that the gleaming new towers would be surrounded by the most appalling slums, reminiscent of the favelas of Rio de Janeiro or the slums of Soweto. The British *Guardian* accepted the article for publication, but did not use it until public opinion was shocked by the death of five African workers, asphyxiated by a makeshift fire in an unventilated shack. Men had to die before the media and French officialdom were willing to take note. Today the Bidonvilles have gone, but immigrants in France still suffer severe housing difficulties. More detail on this is to be found in Chapter 7 of *Immigrant Workers*. Mark Miller describes the subsequent housing struggles of African workers in his book: *Foreign Workers in Western Europe: an Emerging Political Force* (New York, Praeger, 1981).

"The Function of Labor Migration in Western European Capitalism" was written for the British marxist journal *New Left Review* and was reprinted in French and Danish. It was an attempt to provide a theoretical framework based on marxist political economy for understanding labor migration. The central categories used—the industrial reserve army and the labor aristocracy—have given rise to much criticism and controversy. I will return to them in the final chapter of this book.

"Immigrant Workers and Trade Unions in the German Federal Republic," published in several journals and books both in English and in German, was the result of close observation of the wave of strikes led by migrant workers in 1973. This militancy—especially the occupation of the giant Ford plant in Cologne—gave a fright to German employers and authorities, but put the wind up the bureaucratized un-

3

ion apparatus as well. It was one reason for the ban on entry of migrant workers which was suddenly announced in November 1973. This article is in a way a continuation of "The Function of Labor Migration"...centered around a real conflict situation.

"The Social Time-Bomb: Education of an Underclass in West Germany," published in the British journal for black and third-world liberation *Race and Class* in 1980, already belongs to a new epoch: labor migration had been stopped, settlement was obviously taking place, and the "second generation" was becoming a central political concern. Now issues of social integration and public order were coming to the fore—a trend which became more marked throughout Europe after the British riots of 1981.

"The Guest-Worker in Western Europe—an Obituary," written in 1985 from the perspective of my new position in Australia, was meant as my final statement on the system of temporary recruitment in Europe. It was designed to sum up the reasons for the rise and fall of the guest-worker system for an international audience. It should be read as a restatement of the political economy themes raised in "The Function of Labor Migration..." from a different vantage point and over a decade later.

"A New Agenda in Multiculturalism" was written as a contribution to political debates on ethnic affairs policies in Australia in early 1987. Australia has gone much further than most other countries in adopting explicit policies of ethnic pluralism, and also in relating these to measures designed to achieve "social justice" for member of all ethnic communities. However, developments in 1986 appeared to herald a retreat from these policies, and a revival of ethnocentrism in public discourse. The article analyses these trends, and points to their political consequences. Soon after the Labor Government changed their policies again, putting far more emphasis on multiculturalism. Fears of losing the "ethnic vote" appeared to lie behind this trend.

"The Bicentenary and the Failure of Australian Nationalism," written with Bill Cope, Mary Kalantzis and Michael Morrissey of the Centre for Multicultural Studies, was first published in *Race and Class.* It is an essay on the relationship between class, ethnicity and national identity, and is based on our book *Mistaken Identity: Multiculturalism and the Decline of Nationalism in Australia* (Sydney, Pluto Press, 1988). We argue that migration and ethnic diversity are breaking down national boundaries and transforming cultures, creating the potential for a new cosmopolitan society. Australia, as the country with highest ratio of immigrants to population is most advanced along this path, but other countries may follow—unless a new ethnocentrism asserts itself, as the successes of the National Front in France may indicate.

"Global Workforce, Global Economy, Global Culture?" is an essay especially written for this collection. Its aim is to summarize current global trends in migration and ethnic relations.

# Bidonville—A French Word for Hell

The Ministry of the Interior has estimated that there are 75,346 people living in bidonvilles throughout France. A bidonville (the name comes from bidons—petrol cans—hammered flat to provide building material) is a "group of light construction erected on unprepared land, whether closed off or not, with materials found by chance." The official figures probably under-estimate the problem considerably, because bidonville residents often do not give accurate answers to the census-takers as they are afraid of any form of officialdom and their papers are frequently not in order.

Bidonvilles tend to spring up wherever there is a big building project, usually on the outskirts of cities. Thirty-five per cent of building workers in France are foreigners and normal housing is often unobtainable for them. This explains the paradox that bidonvilles are usually near modern housing developments.

When a homeless family or group of male immigrants moves into a bidonville, their first dwelling is often and old truck or bus which has been dumped. At La Courneuve, in the northern suburbs of Paris, whole Yugoslav families with three or four children live in small delivery vans. These are the most recent arrivals.

Once established they collect building materials—corrugated iron, discarded planks, hardboard—and build a shack. Those who have been there longest (up to 15 years in some cases) even have some brick walls. From a high vantage point, the bidonville looks like a rubbish dump, for the inhabitants pile any available material round their walls and on their roofs in a vain attempt to keep out wet and cold.

There are no sanitary amenities of any kind. The open sewers which develop are a constant danger to health. In some areas the local authorities have been persuaded to collect refuse from time to time: in others there is simply an ever-growing heap. At Nanterre one bidonville of more than 1,000 North Africans shares a single water tap with a near-by Portuguese "village."

Once a family has been reduced to living in a bidonville, a vicious circle tends to keep it there. Frequent illness caused by the bad housing conditions, and bad time-keeping caused by lack of transport, make it difficult for a man to keep a good job. Soon, employers come to know the addresses of bidonvilles and will not employ men giving them (which leads to a profitable trade in phoney domicile certificates issued by unscrupulous hoteliers).

Bidonvilles tend to develop their own forms of communal existence, which makes life somewhat less unbearable, but which, on the other hand, causes difficulties with regard to re-housing and integration into French society. To some extent, immigrants living in bidonvilles are

Originally published as "Bidonville—A French Word for Hell." *Manchester Guardian Weekly* 24(1) January, 1970.

able to maintain the patterns of life of their own countries. The men have to adapt to urban-industrial conditions at work, but the bidonville is a ghetto in which they and their families are completely isolated from other aspect of French society.

At Champigny, about 10,000 Portuguese have a completely independent community. Here the shacks are fairly well built. Many have their own water taps outside and most have electricity.

But even where communal solidarity has somewhat improved matters, nobody lives in a bidonville from choice. In the country with the worst housing shortage in Western Europe, the 2.5 million immigrants are at the end of the queue for every type of accommodation. Since the war, French Government policy has encouraged large families and immigration, but has done little to provide housing for the resulting population growth. Today it is estimated that it would be necessary to build 600,000 dwellings (half of them with public money) a year for 20 years to make up the deficiency.

For several years the French Government has carried out a programme for clearing away the bidonvilles through a special fund (*Le fonds d'action sociale pour les travailleurs migrants*—FAS). About two-thirds of the money for this fund comes from the immigrants themselves in the form of deductions from family allowances when the children remain in the country of origin. For example, in 1967 a French worker with five children got Fr.531 a month in family allowances. His Portuguese colleague with five children at home got Fr.89—i.e. the amount he would have been entitled to if working in Portugal. The difference went to the FAS.

Since 1959, the FAS has helped to finance about 60,000 hostel beds for workers whose families are not in France. This is only a faction of the number needed, but even if they do have the opportunity many immigrants are unwilling to move into such hostels.

Apart from restrictions in some hostels (no visitors, lights out at a fixed time), the rent—between 60 and 120 francs a month—is too high for men who have to support families at home. Some hostels are built much too far away from the places of work. Organizations representing immigrants have demanded a say in the running of the FAS, and protest at having to pay twice for the accommodation—once through their compulsory contributions to the FAS and again in the form of rent. The FAS housing programme for single men also creates racial segregation as there are separate hostels for black Africans.

The FAS also gives subsidies to provide family housing for immigrants. But the proportion of foreigners in a housing development is not allowed to exceed 15 per cent to avoid conflict and the growth of separate communities. Often, foreigners from bidonvilles are not immediately re-housed in normal flats, but are sent first to *cites de transit* (transit centers).

The idea is that they are unused to modern urban housing, having come straight from a backward rural area to the bidonville. In the *cite de transit* they are supposed to get used to modern sanitary facilities and housekeeping methods under the guidance of social workers, before moving on to normal flats after a year or two. In fact, immigrant families tend to stay much longer in the *cites*. New flats are just not available for them and there are not enough social workers. The *cites*— usually wooden huts—become forgotten ghettoes, finally to form nuclei for new bidonvilles.

# The Function of Labour Immigration in Western European Capitalism
## *With Godula Kosack*

The domination of the working masses by a small capitalist ruling class has never been based on violence alone. Capitalist rule is based on a range of mechanisms, some objective products of the economic process, others subjective phenomena arising through manipulation of attitudes. Two such mechanisms, which received considerable attention from the founder of scientific socialism, are the industrial reserve army, which belongs to the first category, and the labor aristocracy, which belongs to the second. These two mechanisms are closely related, as are the objective and subjective factors which give rise to them.

Engels pointed out that "English manufacture must have, at all times save the brief periods of highest prosperity, and unemployed reserve army of workers, in order to produce the masses of goods required by the market in the liveliest months."[1] Marx showed that the industrial reserve army or surplus working population is not only the necessary product of capital accumulation and the associated increase in labor productivity, but at the same time "the lever of capitalist accumulation", "a condition of existence of the capitalist mode of production".[2] Only by bringing ever more workers into the production process can the capitalist accumulate capital, which is the precondition for extending production and applying new techniques. These new techniques throw out of work the very men whose labor allowed their application. They are set free to provide a labor reserve which is available to be thrown into other sectors as the interests of the capitalist require. "The whole form of the movement of modern industry depends, therefore, upon the constant transformation of a part of the laboring population into unemployed or half-employed hands."[3] The pressure of the industrial reserve army forces those workers who are employed to accept long hours and poor conditions. Above all "Taking them as a whole, the general movements of wages are exclusively regulated by the expansion and contraction of the industrial reserve army."[4] If employment grows and the reserve army contracts workers are in a better position to demand higher wages. When this happens, profits and capital accumulation diminish, investment falls and men are thrown out of work, leading to a growth of the reserve army and a fall in wages. This is the basis of the capitalist economic cycle. Marx mentions the possibility of the workers seeing through the seemingly natural law of relative over-population, and undermining its effectiveness through trade- union activity directed towards co-operation be-

Originally published in *New Left Review* no. 23 (July 1972): pp.3-21. Reprinted with permission.

tween the employed and the unemployed.[5]

The labor aristocracy is also described by Engels and Marx. By conceding privileges to certain well-organized sectors of labor, above all to craftsmen (who by virtue of their training could not be readily replaced by members of the industrial reserve army), the capitalists were able to undermine class consciousness and secure an opportunist non-revolutionary leadership for these sectors.[6] Special advantages, sometimes taking the form of symbols of higher status (different clothing salary instead of wages, etc) rather than higher material rewards, were also conferred upon foremen and non-manual workers, with the aim of distinguishing them from other workers and causing them to identify their interests with those of the capitalists. Engels pointed out that the privileges given to some British workers were possible because of the vast profits made by the capitalists through domination of the work market and imperialist exploitation of labor in other countries.[7] Lenin emphasized the effects of imperialism on class consciousness: "Imperialism . . . makes it economically possible to bribe the upper strata of the proletariat, and thereby fosters, gives shape to, and strengthen opportunism."[8] ". . . A section of the proletariat allows itself to be led by men bought by, or at least paid by, the bourgeoisie", and the result is a split among the workers and "temporary decay in the working-class movement."[9]

The industrial reserve army and the labor aristocracy have not lost their importance as mechanisms of domination in the current phase of organized monopoly capitalism. However, the way in which they function has undergone important changes. In particular the maintenance of an industrial reserve army within the developed capitalists countries of West Europe has become increasingly difficult. With the growth of the labor movement after the First World War, economic crises and unemployment began to lead to political tensions which threatened the existence of the capitalist system. Capitalism responded by setting up fascist regimes in the areas where it was most threatened, in order to suppress social conflict through violence. The failure of this strategy, culminating in the defeat of fascism in 1945, was accompanied by the reinforcement of the non-capitalist bloc in East Europe and by a further strengthening of the labor movement in West Europe. In order to survive, the capitalist system had to aim for continuous expansion and full employment at any price. But full employment strikes at a basic principle of the capitalist economy: the use of the industrial reserve army to keep wages down and profits up. A substitute for the traditional form of reserve army had to be found, for without it capitalist accumulation is impossible. Moreover, despite Keynsian economics, it is not possible completely to avoid the cyclical development of the capitalist economy. It was therefore necessary to find a way of cushioning the effects of crises, so as to hinder the development of dangerous social tensions.

The solution to these problems adopted by West European capitalism has been the employment of immigrant workers from underdeveloped areas of Southern Europe or from the Third World.[10] Today, the unemployed masses of these areas from a "latent surplus-population"[11] or reserve army, which can be imported into the developed countries as the interests of the capitalist class dictate. In addition to this economic function, the employment of immigrant workers has an important socio-political function for capitalism: by creating a split between immigrant and indigenous workers along national and racial lines and offering better conditions and status to indigenous workers, it is possible to give large sections of the working class the consciousness of a labor aristocracy.

The employment of immigrant workers in the capitalist production process is not a new phenomenon. The Irish played a vital part in British industrialization. Not only did they provide a special form of labor for heavy work of a temporary nature on railways, canals and roads;[12] their competition also forced down wages and conditions for other workers. Engels described Irish immigration as a "cause of abasement to which the English worker is exposed, a cause permanently active in forcing the whole class downwards."[13] Marx described the antagonism between British and Irish workers, artificially created by the mass media of the ruling class, as "the secret of the impotence of the English working class, despite their organization."[14] As industrialization got under way in France, Germany and Switzerland in the latter half of the 19th century, these countries too brought in foreign labor: from Poland, Italy and Spain. There were 800,000 foreign workers in the German Reich in 1907. More than a third of the Ruhr miners were Poles. Switzerland had half a million foreigners in 1910—15 per cent of her total population. French heavy industry was highly dependent on immigrant labor right up to the Second World War. According to Lenin, one of the special features of imperialism was "the decline in emigration from imperialist countries and the increase in immigration into these countries from the more backward countries where lower wages are paid."[15] This was a main cause of the division of the working class. The fascist form of capitalism also developed its own specific form of exploiting immigrant workers: the use of forced labor. No less then 7 1/2 million deportees from occupied countries and prisoners of war were working in Germany by 1944, replacing the men recruited for the army. About a quarter of German munitions production was carried out by foreign labor.[16]

Compared with early patterns, immigration of workers to contemporary West Europe has two new features. The first is its character as a permanent part of the economic structure. Previously, immigrant labor was used more or less temporarily when the domestic industrial reserve army was inadequate for some special reason, like war or unusually fast expansion; since 1945, however, large numbers of immigrant workers have taken up key positions in the productive process, so that even in the case of recession their labor cannot be dispensed with. The second is its importance as the basis of the modern industrial reserve army. Other groups which might conceivably fulfil the same function—non-working women, the disabled and the chronic sick, members of the lumpenproletariat whose conditions prevent them from working[17]—have already been integrated into the production process to the extent to which this is profitable for the capitalist system. The use of further reserves of this type would require costly social measures (e.g. adequate kindergartens). The main traditional form of the industrial reserve army—men thrown out of work by rationalization and cyclical crises—is hardly available today, for reasons already mentioned. Thus immigration is of key importance for the capitalist system.

## The Development of Immigration since 1945

There are around eleven million immigrants[18] living in West Europe, making up about 5 per cent of total population. Relatively few have gone to industrially less developed countries like Norway, Austria and Denmark, while large concentrations are to be found in highly industrialized countries like Belgium, Sweden, West Germany, France, Switzerland and Britain. Our analysis concentrates on the four last-named which have about 90 per cent of all immigrants in West Europe between them.

*Immigrant in West Germany, France, Switzerland and Britain[19]*

|  | Immigrants (thousands) | Immigrants as percentage of total population | Date of figures (latest available) |
| --- | --- | --- | --- |
| West Germany | 2,977 | 4.8 | September 1970 |
| France | 3,177 | 6.4 | December 1969 |
| Switzerland | 972 | 16.0 | December 1969 |
| Britain | 2,603 | 5.0 | December 1966 |

Most immigrants in Germany and Switzerland come from Southern Europe. The main groups in Germany are Italians (574,00 in 1970), Yugoslavs (515,000), Turks (469,000), Greeks (343,000) and Spaniards (246,000). In Switzerland, the Italians are by far the largest group (532,000 in 1969) followed by Germans (116,000) and Spaniards (98,000). France and Britain also have considerable numbers of European immigrants, but in addition large contingents from former colonies in Africa, Asia and the Caribbean. France has 617,000 Spaniards, 612,000 Italians, 480,000 Portuguese, as well as 608,000 Algerians, 143,000 Moroccans, 89,000 Tunisians, about 55,000 black Africans and an unknown number (probably about 200,000) from the remaining colonies (euphemistically referred to as Overseas Departments) in the West Indies and the African island of Réunion. The largest immigrant group in Britain comes from the Irish Republic (739,000 in 1966). Most of the other Europeans were displaced persons and the like who came during and after the war: Germans (142,000) Poles (118,000). Cypriots number 60,000. There are also an increasing number of South Europeans, often allowed in on a short-term basis for work in catering and domestic service. Colored immigrants comprise about one third of the total, the largest groups coming from the West Indies (269,000 in 1966), India (240,000) and Pakistan (75,000).[20]

The migratory movements and the government policies which direct them reflect the growing importance and changing function of immigrant labor in West Europe. Immediately after the Second World War, Switzerland, Britain and France recruited foreign workers. Switzerland needed extra labor for the export boom permitted by her intact industry in the middle of war-torn Europe. The "European Voluntary Workers" in Britain (initially displaced persons, later Italians) were assigned to specific jobs connected with industrial reconstruction. The reconstruction boom was not expected to last. Both Switzerland and Britain imposed severe restrictions of foreign workers, designed to stop them from settling and bringing in their families, so that they could be dismissed and deported at the least sign of recession. France was something of an exception: her immigration policy was concerned not only with labor needs for reconstruction, but also with permanent immigration to counteract the demographic effects of the low-birth rate.

When West German industry got under way again after the 1949 Currency Reform there was at first no need for immigrants from Southern Europe. An excellent industrial reserve army was provided by the seven million expellees from the former Eastern provinces of the Reich and by the three million refugees from East Germany, many of whom were skilled workers. Throughout the fifties, the presence of these reserves kept wage-growth slow and hence provided the basis for the "economic miracle". By the mid-fifties, however, special labor shortages were appearing, first in agriculture and building. It was then that recruitment of foreign workers (initially on a seasonal basis[21]) was started. Here too, an extremely restrictive policy was followed with regard to family entry and long-term settlement. "Rotation" of the foreign labor force was encouraged. In this stage, the use of immigrants in the countries mentioned followed the pre-war pattern: they were brought in to satisfy special and, it was thought, temporary labor needs in certain sectors. They were, as an official of the German employers' association put it, "a mobile labor potential."[22]

By the sixties, the situation was changing. Despite mild cyclical tendencies it was clear that there was not going to be a sudden return to the pre-war boom- slump pattern. The number of immigrant workers grew extremely rapidly in the late fifties and early sixties. Between 1956 and 1965 nearly one millon new workers entered France.

The number of foreign workers in West Germany increased from 279,000 in 1960 to over 1.3 million in 1966. In Switzerland there were 326,000 immigrant workers (including seasonals) in 1956, and 721,000 in 1964. This was also the period of mass immigration to Britain from the Commonwealth.[23] The change was not merely quantitative: immigrants were moving into and becoming indispensable in ever more sectors of the economy. They were no longer filling gaps in peripheral branches like agriculture and building but were becoming a vital part of the labor force in key industries like engineering and chemicals. Moreover, there was growing competition between the different countries to obtain the "most desirable" immigrants, i.e. those with the best education and the least cultural distance from the receiving countries. The growing need for labor was forcing the recruiters to go further and further afield: Turkey and Yugoslavia were replacing Italy as Germany's main labor source. Portugal and North Africa were replacing Italy and Spain in the case of France.

As a result, new policies intended to attract and integrate immigrant workers, but also to control them better, were introduced. One such measure was the free labor movement policy of the EEC, designed to increase the availability of the rural proletariat of Sicily and the Mezzogiorno to West European capital.[24] Germany and Switzerland liberalized the conditions for family entry and long- term settlement, while at the same time tightening political control through measures such as the German 1965 Foreigners Law. France tried to increase control over entries, in order to prevent the large-scale clandestine immigration which had taken place throughout the fifties and sixties (and still does, despite the new policy). At the same time restrictions were made on the permanent settlement of non Europeans—officially because of their "greater difficulties in integrating". In Britain, racialist campaigns led to the stopping of unrestricted Commonwealth immigration in 1962. By limiting the labor supply this measure contradicted the economic interests of the ruling class. The new Immigration Act of 1971, which could provide the basis for organized and controlled labor recruitment of the German and French pattern is a corrective, although its application for this purpose is not required, since the ruling class has created an internal industrial reserve army through unemployment.

In view of the stagnant domestic labor force potential and the long-term growth trend of the economy, immigrant labor has become a structural necessity for West European capitalism.[25] It has a dual function today.[26] One section is maintained as a mobile fluctuating labor force, which can be moved from factory to factory or branch to branch as required by the development of the means of production, and which can be thrown out of work and deported as required without causing social tensions. This function was shown clearly by the West German recession of 1966-7, when the foreign labor force dropped by 400,000, although there were never more than 29,000 receiving unemployment benefit. As a United Nations study pointed out, West Germany was able to export unemployment to the home countries of the migrants.[27] The other section is required for permanent employment throughout the economy. They are offered better conditions and the chance of long-term settlement.[28] Despite this they fulfil the function of an industrial reserve army, for they are given inferior jobs, have no political rights and may be used as a constant threat to the wages and conditions of the local labor force.

## Occupational Position

The immigrant percentage of the population given in the table above in no way reflects the contribution of immigrants to the economy. They are mainly young men, whose dependents are sent for later if at all. Many of them remain only a few years, and are then replaced by others, so that there are hardly any retired immigrants. Immigrants therefore have higher than average rates of economic activity, and make contributions to health, unemployment and pension insurance far in excess of their demands on such schemes.[29] Particularly high rates of activity are to be found among recently arrived groups, or among those who for social and cultural reasons, tend not to bring dependents with them: Portuguese and North Africans in France, Turks in Germany and Pakistanis in Britain. Immigrant workers are about 6.5 per cent of the labor force in Britain, 7-8 per cent in France, 10 per cent in West Germany and 30 per cent in Switzerland. Even these figures do not show adequately the structural importance of immigrant labor, which is concentrated in certain areas and types of work.

The overwhelming majority of immigrants live in highly industrialized and fast- growing urban areas like Paris, the Lyon region, the Ruhr, Baden-W rttemberg, London and the West Midlands. For example 31.2 per cent of all immigrants in France live in the Paris region, compared with only 19.2 per cent of the total population. 9.5 per cent of the inhabitant of the Paris region are immigrants.[30] In Britain more than one third of all immigrants are to be found in Greater London compared with one sixth of the total population. Immigrants make up 12 per cent of London's population.[31]

More important still is the concentration in certain industries. Switzerland is the extreme case: the whole industrial sector is dominated by foreign workers who make up more than 40 per cent of the factory labor force. In many branches- -for instance textiles, clothing, building and catering—they outnumber Swiss employees.[32] Of the nearly two million foreign workers in Germany in September 1970, 38.5 per cent were in the metal-producing and engineering industry, 24.2 in other manufacturing branches and 16.7 per cent in building. Foreign workers accounted for 13.7 per cent of total employment in metal producing and engineering. The proportion was even higher in some industries with particularly bad working conditions, like plastic, rubber and asbestos manufacture (18.4 per cent). In building, foreign workers were 17.5 per cent of the labor force. On the other hand they made up only 3.4 per cent of all employees in the services, although their share was much higher in catering (14.8 per cent).[33] Similar concentrations were revealed by the 1968 Census in France: 35.6 per cent of immigrant men were employed in building and 13.5 per cent in engineering and electrical goods. 28.8 per cent of foreign women were domestic servants. In Britain the concentration of immigrants in certain industries is less marked, and different immigrant groups have varying patterns. The Irish are concentrated in construction, while Commonwealth immigrants are over-represented in metal manufacture and transport. Pakistani men are mainly to be found in the textile industry and Cypriots in clothing and footwear and in distribution. European immigrants are frequently in the services sector. Immigrant women of all nationalities tend to work in services, although some groups (Cypriots, West Indians) also often work in manufacturing.[34]

In general immigrants are concentrated in certain basic industries, where they form a high proportion of the labor force. Together with their geographical concentration this means that immigrant workers are of great importance in the very types of enterprise and areas which used to be regarded as the strongholds of the class-conscious proletariat. The real concentration is even greater than the figures show, for within each industry the immigrants tend to have become predominant in certain departments and occupations. There can be hardly a foundry in West Europe in which immigrants do not form a majority, or at least a high proportion, of the labor force. The same applies to monotonous production line work, such as car-assembly. Renault, Citroen, Volkswagen, Ford of Cologne and Opel all have mainly foreign workers on the assembly line (The British motor industry is an exception in this respect).

Perhaps the best indication of the occupational concentration of the immigrant labor force is given by their socio-economic distribution. For instance a survey carried out in 1968 in Germany showed that virtually no Southern Europeans are in non-manual employment. Only between 7 per cent and 16 per cent of the various nationalities were skilled workers while between 80 per cent and 90 per cent were either semi-skilled or unskilled.[35] By comparison about a third of German workers are non-manual, and among manual workers between one third and one half are in the skilled category in the various industries. In France a survey carried out at Lyon in 1967 found that where they worked in the same industry, the French were mainly in managerial, non-manual or skilled occupations, while the immigrants were concentrated in manual occupations, particularly semi-skilled and unskilled ones. The relegation to unskilled jobs is particularly marked for North Africans and Portuguese.[36] In Britain, only about 26 per cent of the total labor force falls into the unskilled and semi-skilled manual categories, but the figure is 42 per cent for the Irish, 50 per cent for the Jamaicans, 65 per cent for the Pakistanis and 55 per cent for the Italians.[37]

Immigrants form the lowest stratum of the working class carrying out unskilled and semi-skilled work in those industrial sectors with the worst working conditions and/or the lowest pay.[38] The entry of immigrants at the bottom of the labor market has made possible the release of many indigenous workers from such employment, and their promotion to jobs with better conditions and higher status, i.e. skilled, supervisory or white-collar employment. Apart from the economic effects, this process has a profound impact on the class consciousness of the indigenous workers concerned. That will be discussed in more detail below.

*Social Position*

The division of the working class within the production process is duplicated by the division in other spheres of society. The poor living conditions of immigrants have attracted too much liberal indignation and welfare zeal to need much description here. Immigrants get the worst types of housing: in Britain slums and run-down lodging houses, in France *bidonvilles* (shanty-towns) and overcrowded hotels, in Germany and Switzerland camps of wooden huts belonging to the employers and attics in the cities. It is rare for immigrants to get council houses. Immigrants are discriminated against by many landlords, so that those who do specialize in housing them can charge extortionate rents for inadequate facilities. In Germany and France, official programmes have been established to provide hostel accommodation for single immigrant workers. These hostels do provide somewhat better material conditions. On the other hand they increase the segregation of immigrant workers from the rest of the working class, deny them any private life, and above all put them under the control of the employers 24 hours a day.[39] In Germany the employers have repeatedly attempted to use control over immigrants' accommodation to force them to act as strike-breakers.

Language and vocational training courses for immigrant workers are generally provided only when it is absolutely necessary for the production process, as in mines for example. Immigrant children are also at a disadvantage: they tend to live in run-down overcrowded areas where school facilities are poorest. No adequate measures are taken to deal with their special educational problems (e.g. language difficulties), so that their educational performance is usually below-average. As a result of their bad working and living conditions, immigrants have serious health problems. For instance they have much higher tuberculosis rates than the rest of the population virtually everywhere.[40] As there are health controls at the borders, it is clear that such illnesses have been contracted in West Europe rather than being brought in by the immigrants.

The inferior work-situation and living conditions of immigrants have caused some bourgeois sociologists to define them as a "lumpenproletariat" or a "marginal group". This is clearly incorrect. A group which makes up 10, 20 or 30 per cent of the industrial labor force cannot be regarded as marginal to society. Others speak of a "new proletariat" or a "sub-proletariat". Such terms are also wrong.

The first implies that the indigenous workers have ceased to be proletarians and have been replaced by the immigrants in this social position. The second postulates that immigrant workers have a different relationship to the means of production that traditionally characteristic of the proletariat. In reality both indigenous and immigrant workers share the same relationship to the means of production: they are excluded from ownership or control; they are forced to sell their labor power in order to survive; they work under the direction and in the interests of others. In the sphere of consumption both categories of workers are subject to the laws of the commodity market, where the supply and price of goods is determined not by their use value but by the profitability for capitalists; both are victims of landlords, retail monopolists and similar bloodsuckers and manipulators of the consumption-terror. These are the characteristics typical of the proletariat ever since the industrial revolution, and on this basis immigrant and indigenous workers must be regarded as members of the same class: the proletariat. But it is a divided class: the marginal privileges conceded to indigenous workers and the particularly intensive exploitation of immigrants combine to create a barrier between the two groups, which appear as distinct strata within the class. The division is deepened by certain legal, political and psychological factors, which will be discussed below.

*Discrimination*

Upon arrival in West Europe, immigrants from under-developed areas have little basic education or vocational training, and are usually ignorant of the language. They know nothing of prevailing markets conditions or prices. In capitalist society, these characteristics are sufficient to ensure that immigrants get poor jobs and social conditions. After a period of adaptation to industrial work and urban life, the prevailing ideology would lead one to expect many immigrants to obtain better jobs, housing, etc. Special mechanisms ensure that this does not happen in the majority of cases. On the one hand there is institutionalized discrimination in the form of legislation which restricts immigrants' civic and labor market rights. On the other hand there are informal discriminatory practices based on racialism or xenophobia.

In nearly all West European countries, labor market legislation discriminates against foreigners. They are granted labor permits for a specific job in a certain firm for a limited period. They do not have the right to move to better-paid or more highly qualified positions, at least for some years. Workers who change jobs without permission are often deported. Administrative practices in this respect have been liberalized to some extent in Germany and Switzerland in recent years, due to the need for immigrant labor in a wider range of occupations, but the basic restrictiveness of the system remains. In Britain, Commonwealth immigrants (once admitted to the country) and the Irish had equal rights with local workers until the 1971 Immigration Act. now Commonwealth immigrants will have the same labor market situation as aliens. The threat of deportation if an immigrant loses his job is a very powerful weapon for the employer. Immigrants who demand better conditions can be sacked for undiscipline and the police will do the rest.[41] Regulations which restrict family entry and permanent settlement also keep immigrants in inferior positions. If a man may stay only for a few years, it is not worth his while to learn the language and take vocational courses.

Informal discrimination is well known in Britain, where it takes the form of the color bar. The PEP study[42], as well as many other investigations, has shown that colored immigrants encounter discrimination with regard to employment, housing and the provision of serviced such as mortgages and insurance. The more qualified a colored man is, the more likely he is to encounter discrimination. This mechanism keeps immigrants in "their place", i.e. doing the dirty, unpleasant jobs. Immigrants in the other European countries also encounter informal discrimination. Immigrants rarely get promotion to supervisory or nonmanual jobs, even when they are well qualified. Discrimination in housing is widespread. In Britain, adverts specifying "no colored" are forbidden, but in Germany or Switzerland one still frequently sees "no foreigners".

The most serious form of discrimination against immigrant workers is their deprivation of political rights. Foreigners may not vote in local or national elections. Nor may they hold public office, which in France is defined so widely as to include trade-union posts. Foreigners do not generally have the same rights as local workers with regard to eligibility for works councils and similar representative bodies. The main exception to this formal exclusion from political participation concerns Irish and Commonwealth immigrants in Britain, who do have the right to vote (the same will not apply to those who enter under the 1971 Act). But the Mangrove case shows the type of repression which may be expected by any immigrants who dare to organize themselves. Close police control over the political activities of immigrants is the rule throughout Europe, and deportation of political and trade-union militants is common. After the May Events in France, hundreds of foreign workers were deported.[43] Foreign language newspapers of the CGT labor federation have been repeatedly forbidden. The German Foreigners Law of 1965 lays down that the political activity of foreigners can be forbidden if "important interests of the German Federal Republic require this"—a provision so flexible that the police can prevent any activity they choose. Even this is not regarded as sufficient. When Federal Chancellor Willy Brandt visited Iran in March 1972 to do an oil deal, the Shah complained strongly about Iranian students being allowed to criticize him in Germany. The Greek and Yugoslav ambassadors have also protested about the activities of their citizens. Now the German Government is working on a new law which would go so far as to make police permission necessary even for private meetings of foreigners in closed rooms.[44]

Discrimination against immigrants is a reflection of widespread hostility towards them. In Britain, this is regarded as "color prejudice" or "racialism", and indeed there can be no doubt that the hostility of large sections of the population is at present directed against black people. Race relations theorists attribute the problems connected with immigration partly to the immigrant's difficulties in adapting to the prevailing norms of the "host society"; and partly to the indigenous population's inbred distrust of the newcomers who can be distinguished by their skin color. The problems are abstracted from the socioeconomic structure and reduced to the level of attitudes. Solutions are to be sought not through political action, but through psychological and educational strategies.[45] But a comparison of surveys carried out in different countries shows that hostility towards immigrants is everywhere as great as in Britain, even where the immigrants are white.[46] The Italian who moves to the neighboring country of Switzerland is as unpopular as the Asian in Britain. This indicates that hostility is based on the position of immigrants in society and not on the color of their skin.

Racialism and xenophobia are products of the capitalist national state and of its imperialist expansion.[47] Their principal historical function was to split the working class on the international level, and to motivate one section to help exploit another in the interests of the ruling class. Today such ideologies help to deepen the split within the working class in West Europe. Many indigenous workers do not perceive that they share a common class position and class interests with immigrant workers. The basic fact of having the same relationship to the means of production is obscured by the local workers' marginal advantages with regard to material conditions and status. The immigrants are regarded not as class comrades, but as alien intruders who pose an economic and social threat. It is feared that they will take away the jobs of local labor, that they will be used by the employers to force down wages and to break strikes.[48] Whatever the behavior of the immigrant workers—and in fact they almost invariably show solidarity with their indigenous colleagues—such fears are not without a basis. It is indeed the strategy of the employers to use immigration to put pressure on wages and to weaken the labor movement.[49] The very social and legal weakness of the immigrants is a weapon in the hands of the employers. Other points of competition are to be found outside work, particularly on the housing market. The presence of immigrants is often regarded as the cause of rising rents and increased overcrowding in the cities. By making immigrants the scapegoats for the insecurity and inadequate conditions which the capitalist system inevitably provides for workers, attention is diverted from the real causes.

Workers often adopt racialism as a defence mechanism against a real or apparent threat to their conditions. It is an incorrect response to a real problem. By preventing working-class unity, racialism assists the capitalists in their strategy of "divide and rule". The function of racialism in the capitalist system is often obscured by the fact that racialist campaigns usually have petty-bourgeois leadership and direct their slogans against the big industrialists. The Schwarzenbach Initiative in Switzerland—which called for the deportation of a large proportion of the immigrant population—is an example,[50] as are Enoch Powell's campaigns for repatriation. Such demands are opposed by the dominant sections of the ruling class. The reason is clear: a complete acceptance of racialism would prevent the use of immigrants as an industrial reserve army. But despite this, racialist campaigns serve the interests of the ruling class: they increase tension between indigenous and immigrant workers and weaken the labor movement. The large working-class following gained by Powell in his racialist campaigns demonstrates how dangerous they are. Paradoxically, their value for capitalism lies in their very failure to achieve their declared aims.

The presence of immigrant workers is one of the principal factors contributing to the lack of class consciousness among large sections of the working class. The existence of a new lower stratum of immigrants changes the worker's perception of his own position in society. Instead of a dichotomic view of society, in which the working masses confront a small capitalist ruling class, many workers now see themselves as belonging to an intermediate stratum, superior to the unskilled immigrant workers. Such a consciousness is typified by an hierarchical view of society and by orientation towards advancement through individual achievement and competition, rather than through solidarity and collective action. This is the mentality of the labor aristocracy and leads to opportunism and the temporary decay of the working-class movement.

### Immigration and Society

The impact of immigration on contemporary West european society may now be summarized.

*Economic effects:* the new industrial reserve army of immigrant workers is a major stabilizing factor of the capitalist economy. By restraining wage increases, immigration is a vital precondition for capital accumulation and hence for growth. In the long run, wages may grow more in a country which has large-scale immigration than in one which does not, because of the dynamic effect of increased capital accumulation on productivity. However, wages are a smaller share, and profits a larger share of national income than would have been the case without immigration.[51] The best illustration of this effect is obtained by comparing the German and the British economies since 1945. Germany has had large and continuous increases in labor force due to immigration. At first wages were held back. The resulting capital accumulation allowed fast growth and continuous rationalization. Britain has had virtually no growth in labor force due to migration (immigration has been cancelled out by emigration of British people to Australia, etc). Every phase of expansion has collapsed rapidly as wages rose due to labor shortages. The long-term effect has been stagnation. By the sixties, German wages overtook those of Britain, while economic growth and rationalization continued at an almost undiminished rate.

*Social effects:* the inferior position of immigrant workers with regard to employment and social conditions has led to a division of the working class into two strata. The split is maintained by various forms of discrimination and is reinforced by racialist and xenophobic ideologies, which the ruling class can disseminate widely through its hegemony over the means of socialization and communication. Large sections of the indigenous workers take the position of a labor aristocracy, which objectively participates in the exploitation of another group of workers.

*Political effects:* the decline of class consciousness weakens the working- class movement. In addition, the denial of political rights to immigrants excludes a large section of the working class from political activity, and hence weakens the class as a whole. The most exploited section of the working class is rendered voiceless and powerless. Special forms of repression are designed to keep it that way.

## Working-class Movement and Immigrant Labor

Immigrant labor has an important function for contemporary West European capitalism. This does not mean, however, that socialists should oppose labor migration as such. To do so would be incorrect for two reasons. Firstly, it would contradict the principle of proletarian internationalism, which rejects the maintenance of privileges for one section of the working class at the expense of another. Secondly, opposition to immigration would cause immigrants in West Europe to regard the working-class movement as its enemy, and would therefore deepen the split in the working class—which is exactly what the capitalists are hoping for. The aim of a socialist policy on immigration must be to overcome the split in the working class by bringing immigrant workers into the labor movement and fighting against the exploitation to which they are subjected. Only by demanding full economic, social and political equality for immigrants can we prevent the employers form using them as a weapon against working-class interests.

The policies of the trade unions with regard to immigration have varied widely. The Swiss unions oppose immigration, and have since the mid-fifties campaigned for a reduction in the number of foreign workers. At the same time, they claim to represent all workers, and call upon foreigners to join—not surprisingly, with little success. The British unions opposed the recruitment of European Voluntary Workers after the war, and insisted upon collective agreements limiting their rights to promotion, laying down that they should be dismissed first in case of redundancy and so on.[52] The policy towards Commonwealth immigration has been totally different: the TUC has opposed immigration control, and rejected any form of discrimination. This rejection has, however, been purely verbal, and virtually nothing has been done to organize immigrants or to counter the special forms of exploitation to which they are subject. The CGT in France opposed immigration completely during the late forties and the fifties, condemning is as an instrument designed to attack French workers' conditions. More recently the CGT, as well as the two other big labor federations, the CFDT and the FO, have come to regard immigration as inevitable. All have special secretariats to deal with immigrant workers' problems and do everything possible to bring them into the unions. In Germany, the DGB has accepted immigration and has set up offices to advise and help immigrants. The member unions also have advisory services, and provide foreign language bulletins and special training for immigrant shop-stewards. In general, those unions which have recognized the special problems of immigration have not done so on the basis of a class analysis (here the CGT is to some extent an exception). Rather they have seen the problems on a humanitarian level, they have failed to explain the strategy of the employers to the workers, and the measures taken have been of a welfare type, designed to integrate immigrants socially, rather than to bring them into the class struggle.

Therefore, the unions have succeeded neither in countering racialism among indigenous workers, nor in bringing the immigrant workers into the labor movement on a large scale. The participation of immigrant workers in the unions is on the whole relatively low. This is partly attributable to their rural background and lack of industrial experience, but in addition immigrants often find that the unions do not adequately represent their interests. The unions are controlled by indigenous workers, or by functionaries originating from this group. In situations where immigrant and indigenous workers do not have the same immediate interests (this happens not infrequently due to the differing occupational positions of the two groups, for instance in the question of wage- differentials), the unions tend to take the side of the indigenous workers. Where immigrants have taken action against special forms of discrimination, they have often found themselves deserted by the unions.[53] In such circumstances it is not surprising if immigrants do not join the unions, which they regard as organizations for local labor only. This leads to a considerable weakening of the unions. In Switzerland many unions fear for their very existence, and see the only solution in the introduction of compulsory "solidarity contributions", to be deducted from wages by the employers. In return the unions claim to be the most effective instrument for disciplining the workers. When the employers gave way to a militant strike of Spanish workers in Geneva in 1970, the unions publicly attacked them for making concessions.

Where the unions do not adequately represent immigrant workers. it is sometimes suggested that the immigrants should form their own unions. In fact they have not done so anywhere in contemporary West Europe. This shows a correct class position on their part: the formation of immigrant unions would deepen and institutionalize the split in the working class, and would therefore serve the interests of the employers.[54] On the other hand, all immigrant groups do have their own organizations, usually set up on the basis of nationality, and having social, cultural and political functions. These organizations do not compete with the trade unions, but rather encourage their members to join them. The aims of the political groups have so far been concerned mainly with their countries of origin. They have recruited and trained cadres to combat the reactionary regimes upon returning home. At present, as a result of greater length of stay and increasing problems in West Europe, many immigrant political groups are turning their attention to class struggle in the countries where they work.

It is the task of the revolutionary movement in West Europe to encourage this tendency, by making contact with immigrant groups, assisting them in coordinating with immigrants of other nationalities and with the working-class movement in general, giving help in political education and cadre-training, and carrying out joint actions. Such co-operation means surmounting many problems. Firstly, language and culture may make communication difficult. Secondly, the risk of repression to which immigrant militant are exposed may make them reluctant to make contacts. Thirdly, the experience of discrimination may cause immigrants to distrust all local people. This leads in many cases to cultural nationalism, particularly marked for historical reasons among black people. In order to overcome these difficulties, it is essential for indigenous political groups to study the problems of immigrants and the special forms of discrimination and exploitation to which they are exposed. Concrete attempts to combat these must be made. Indigenous groups must offer co-operation and assistance to immigrants in their struggle, rather than offering themselves as a leadership.

It is not only when revolutionary groups are actively trying to co-operate with immigrant workers' organizations that they come up against the problems of immigration. The majority of immigrants are not politically organized, whether through apathy or fear of repression. Groups agitating in factories or carrying out rent campaigns are likely to come up against large numbers of unorganized immigrants in the course of their daily work. It is then essential to take special steps to communicate with the immigrants and to bring them into the general movement. Failure to do so may result in the development of petty- bourgeois chauvinism within the factory or housing groups, which would correspond precisely with the political aims of the capitalists with regard to labor migration. In Germany, the large numbers of revolutionary groups at present agitating in factories almost invariably find it necessary to learn about the background and problems of immigrant workers, to develop special contacts with them, and to issue leaflets in the appropriate languages. The same applies to housing groups, which frequently find that immigrants form the most under-privileged group in the urban areas where they are working.

Immigrant workers can become a class-conscious and militant section of the labor movement. This has been demonstrated repeatedly;

immigrant workers have played a leading part in strike movements throughout West Europe. They are at present in the forefront of the movement which is occupying empty houses in German cities. Immigrant workers showed complete solidarity with the rest of the working class in May 1968 in France, they were militant in strikes and demonstrations and developed spontaneous forms of organization in the struggle.

But such successes should not make us forget the capitalist strategy behind labor migration. Powerful structural factors connected with the function of immigrants as an industrial reserve army, and with the tendency of part of the indigenous working class to take on the characteristics of a labor aristocracy, lead to a division between immigrant and indigenous workers. Solidarity between these two sections does not come automatically. It requires a correct understanding of the problems within the revolutionary movement and a strategy for countering ruling-class aims. It is necessary to assist the immigrant workers in fighting exploitation and in defending their special interests. At the same time revolutionary groups must combat racialist and xenophobic ideologies within the working class. These are the pre-conditions for developing class-consciousness and bringing the immigrant workers into the class struggle.

## Notes

1. Engels, "The Condition of the Working Class in England", in Marx and Engels, *Britain*, Moscow 1962, p. 119.
2. Marx, *Capital*, Vol. I, Moscow 1961, p. 632.
3. Ibid, p. 633.
4. Ibid., p. 637.
5. Ibid., p. 640.
6. Engels, Preface to the English edition of "The Condition of the Working Class in England", op. cit., p. 28.
7. Engels, "The English Election", in *On Britain*, op. cit., p. 505.
8. Lenin, *Imperialism—the highest State of Capitalism*, Moscow 1966, pp. 96-7.
9. Ibid., pp. 99-100.
10. In this article we examine the function of labor migration only for the countries of immigration. Migration also plays an important stabilizing role for the reactionary regimes of the countries of origin—a role which is understood and to some extent planned by the ruling class in West Europe. Although we are concerned only with West Europe in this article, it is important to note that the use of certain special categories of workers, who can be discriminated against without arousing general solidarity from other workers, is a general feature of modern capitalism. The blacks and chicanos are the industrial reserve army of the USA, the Africans of white-dominated Southern Africa. Current attempts by "liberal" capitalists to relax the color bar to allow blacks into certain skilled and white-collar jobs, both in the USA and South Africa, however estimable in humanitarian terms, are designed mainly to weaken the unions and put pressure on wages in these sectors.
11. Marx mentions several forms taken by the industrial reserve army. One is the "latent" surplus-population of agricultural laborers, whose wages and conditions have been depressed to such an extent that they are merely waiting for a favorable opportunity to move into industry and join the urban proletariat. (*Capital*, Vol., I., op. cit., p. 642.) Although these workers are not yet in industry, the possibility that they may at any time join the industrial labor force increases the capitalist's ability to resist wage increases. The latent industrial reserve army has the same

effect as the urban unemployed. Unemployed workers in other countries, in so far as they may be brought into the industrial labor force whenever required, clearly form a latent industrial reserve army in the same way as rural unemployed within the country.

12. See E. P. Thompson, *The Making of the English Working Class,* Harmondsworth 1968, pp. 469-85.

13. "The Condition of the working Class in England," op. cit., p. 552.

14. Letter to S. Meyer and A. Vogt, 9 April 1870, in *On Britain,* op. cit., p. 552.

15. *Imperialism,* op. cit., p. 98.

16. Hans Pfahlmann, *Fremdarbeiter und Kriegsgefangene in der deutschen Kriegswirtschaft, 1939-1945,* Darmstadt 1968, p. 232.

17. For the role of the lumpenproletariat in the industrial reserve army, see *Capital,* Vol. I, op. cit. p. 643.

18. We use "immigrants" in a broad sense to include all persons living in a West European country which is not their country of birth. Much migration is of a temporary nature, for a period of 3-10 years. But such temporary migration has effects similar to permanent migration when the returning migrant is replaced by a countrymen with similar characteristics. Such migrants may be regarded as a permanent social group with rotating membership.

19. For sources, as well as detailed analysis of social conditions of immigrants, see *Western Europe,* London, Oxford University press for Institute of Race Relations, 1972 (forthcoming).

20. The 1966 Census figures are at present the most recent ones available. It should, however, be noted that, for technical reasons, they seriously under-enumerate the Commonwealth immigrants in Britain. Moreover, the number has grown considerably since 1966, particularly if we look at the whole community including children born to Commonwealth immigrants in Britain, who were not counted by the census. We shall have to wait for the results of the 1971 Census to obtain a more accurate picture of the immigrant population in Britain.

21. Many foreign workers are still employed on a seasonal basis in building, agriculture and catering in France and Switzerland. This is a special form of exploitation. The worker has no income in the off-season and is therefore forced to work very long hours when he does have work. He cannot bring his family with him, he has even more limited civic rights than other immigrants, and he has absolutely no security, for there is no guarantee that his employment will be continued from year to year.

22. Ulrich Freiherr von Gienanth, in *Der Arbeitgeber,* Vol. 18, 20 March 1966, p. 153.

23. For Commonwealth immigration see E.J.B. Rose et al., *Color and Citizenship,* London 1969.

24. Eurocrats refer to the free movement policy as the beginning of a "European labour market". But although EEC citizens have the right to choose which country to be exploited in, they lack any civic or political rights once there. Moreover, the Southern Italian labor reserves are being absorbed by the monopolies of Turin and Milan, so that intra-EEC migration is steadily declining in volume, while migration from outside the EEC increases.

25. Where formalized economic planning exists, this necessity has been publicly formulated. Prognoses on the contribution of immigrants to the labor force were included in the Fourth and Fifth Five-Year Plans in France, and play an even more prominent part in the current Sixth Plan. See *Le VIe plan et les travailleurs étrangers,* Paris 1971.

26. Cf. Ruth Becker, Gerhard D rr, K. H. Tjaden, "Fremdarbeiterbeschäftigung im deutschen Kapitalismus", *Das Argument,* December 1971, p.753.

27. United Nations Economic Commission for Europe, *Economic Survey of Europe 1967,* Geneva 1968, Chapter I,p.49.

28. The distinction between the two sections of the immigrant labor force is formalized in the new French immigration policy introduced in 1968. There are separate regulations for South Europeans, who are encouraged to bring in their families and settle permanently, and Africans (particularly Algerians) who are meant to come for a limited period only, without dependents.

29. It is estimated that foreign workers in Germany are at present paying about 17 per cent of all contributions to pension insurance, but that foreigners are receiving only 0.5 per cent of the total benefits. Heinz Salowsky, "Sozialpolitische Aspekte der Auslanderbeschaftigung", *Berichte des Deutschen Industrie instituts zur Sozialpolitik,* Vol.6 (S), No.2, February 1972, pp. 16-22.
30. Calculated from: "Statistiques du Ministère de l'Intérieur", *Hommes et Migrations: Documents,* No. 788, 15 May 1970; and *Annuaire Statistique de la France 1968.*
31. 1966 Census.
32. *Statistisches Jahrbuch der Schweiz 1967,* pp. 140-1.
33. *Ausländische Arbeitnehmer 1970,* Nürnberg 1971.
34. 1966 Census. For a detailed analysis of immigrants' employment see: K. Jones and A.D. Smith, *The Economic Impact of Commonwealth Immigration,* Cambridge 1970. Also Castles and Kosack, *Immigrant Workers and Class Structure in Western Europe,* Ch.III.
35. *Ausländische Arbeitnehmer 1969,* Nürnberg 1970, p.86.
36. 'L'insertion sociale des étrangers dans l'aire métropolitaine Lyon-Saint-Étienne', *Hommes et Migrations,* No.113, 1969, p.112.
37. 1966 Census.
38. Some employers—particularly small inefficient ones—specialize in the exploitation of immigrants. For instance they employ illegal immigrants, who can be forced to work for very low wages and cannot complain to the authorities for fear of deportation. Such cases often cause much indignation in the liberal and social-democratic press. But, in fact, it is the big efficient firms exploiting immigrants in a legal and relatively humane way which make the biggest profits out of them. The function of immigration in West European capitalism is created not by the malpractices of backward firms (many of whom incidentally could not survive without immigration labor), but by the most advanced sectors of big industry which plan and utilize the position of immigrant workers to their own advantage.
39. "So far as we are concerned, hostel and works represent parts of a single whole. The hostels belong to the mines, so the foreign workers are in our charge from start to finish", stated a representative of the German mining employers proudly. *Magnet Bundesrepublik,* Informationstagung der Bundesvereinigung Deutscher Arbeitgeberverbände, Bonn 1966, p.81.
40. A group of French doctors found that the TB rate for black Africans in the Paris suburb of Montreuil was 156 times greater than that of the local population. R.D. Nicoladze, C. Rendu, G. Millet, "Coupable d'être malades', *Droit et Liberté,* No. 280, March 1969, p.8. For further examples see Castles and Kosack, *Immigrant Workers and Class Structure in Western Europe,* op. cit., Ch.VIII.
41. For a description of how a strike of Spanish workers in a steel-works was broken by the threat of deportation, see P. Gavi, *Les Ouvriers,* Paris 1970, pp. 225-6.
42. W.W. Daniels, *Racial Discrimination in England,* based on the PEP Report, Harmondsworth 1968.
43. See *Review of the International Commission of Jurists,* No. 3, September 1969, and *Migration Today,* No. 13, Autumn 1969.
44. Cf. *Der Spiegel,* No. 7, 7 February 1972
45. See Mark Abrams' study on prejudice in *Color and Citizenship,* pp. 551-604. The results of the study are very interesting, but require careful interpretation. The interpretation given by Abrams is extremely misleading. The results of the prejudice study, which was said to indicate a very low level of prejudice in Britain, attracted more public attention than all the other excellent contributions in this book. For a reanalysis of Abrams' material see Christopher Bagley, *Social Structure and Prejudice in five English Boroughs,* London 1970.
46. We have attempted such comparison in *Immigrant Workers and Class Structure in Western Europe,* Chapter IX. Historical comparisons also tend to throw doubt on the importance of race as a cause of prejudice: white immigrants like the Irish were in the past received just as hostilely as the black immigrants today.
47. Oliver Cromwell Cox, *Caste, Class and Race,* New York 1970, p.317 ff. This superb work of Marxist scholarship is recommended to anyone interested in racialism.

48. Surveys carried out in Germany in 1966 show a growth of hostility towards immigrants. This was directly related to the impending recession and local labor's fear of unemployment.

49. Historically, the best example of this strategy was the use of successive waves of immigrants to break the nascent labor movement in the USA and to follow extremely rapid capital accumulation. *The Jungle* by Upton Sinclair gives an excellent account of this. Similar was the use of internal migrants (the "Okies") in California in the thirties—see John Steinbeck, *The Grapes of Wrath.*

50. Although the Federal Council, the Parliament, the employers, the unions and all the major parties called for rejection of the Schwarzenbach Initiative, it was defeated only by a small majority: 46 per cent of voters supported the Initiative and 54 per cent voted against it.

51. Many bourgeois economists and some *soi-disant* Marxists think that immigra:ion hinders growth because cheap labor reduces the incentive for rationalization. Bourgeois economists may be excused for not knowing (or not admitting) that cheap labor must be the source for the capital which makes rationalization possible. Marxists ought to know it. A good study on the economic impact of immigration is: C.P. Kindleberger, *Europe's Postwar Growth—the Role of Labour Supply,* Cambridge (Mass.) 1967.

52. See Bob Hepple. *Race, Jobs and the Law in Britain,* London 1968, p.50 and Appendix

53. For details of such cases see Castles and Kosack, *Immigrant Workers and Class Structure in Western Europe,* Chapter IV.

54. We do not wish to imply that it is always incorrect for minority groups to form new unions, if the existing ones are corrupt and racialist. It was obviously necessary for militant blacks in the USA to do this, as the existing union structure was actively assisting in their oppression. But organizations like the Detroit Revolutionary Union Movement (DRUM), though consisting initially of blacks only, were not separatist.

# Immigrant Workers and Trade Unions in the German Federal Republic
## *with Godulka Kosak*

*Preliminary Remarks*

The manuscript of the present article was completed in February 1974. It was written under the influence of two important events in the summer of autumn of 1973: the wave of strikes in which immigrant workers played a major part, and the stopping of labor recruitment to Germany in November, ostensibly because of the "oil crisis" Now, a year later, it has become obvious not only that these events are interconnected, but also that they represent a turning point in West German immigration policy. A complete or partial ban on immigration of workers (except from members of the European Community) is likely to be a long-term feature of German economic policy. Why has the importation of labor—so long a major factor in West Germany's economic expansion—ceased to be necessary or profitable to the capitalist class?

In brief, there are two main reasons. First, the West German economy is coming into the phase of "stagflation" which has been characteristic of the U.S.A. and Britain for some years already. Seasonally adjusted unemployment is at its highest level since the early fifties, while the inflation rate hardly drops below last year's peak. Any measures taken to ease unemployment will increase the rate of inflation, thus further eroding the already much reduced international competitiveness of West German products. (A dramatic example of this is the fact that Volkswagen is considering building a plant in the U.S.A., because wage rises in Germany and changes in international exchange rate now make production costs lower there than at home.) The need for new immigrant labor is therefore likely to be small in the near future.

Secondly, the economic and political advantages of cheap immigrant labor have declined in recent years. One reason for this is that the competition between Germany, Switzerland, France, Sweden, etc. for workers during the boom years of the mid-sixties forced concessions with regard to family entry and social provisions, which have necessitated social investments. To avoid misunderstandings: immigrants still have far worse conditions than most indigenous workers and many necessary social facilities are not provided, but the old situation of bringing in masses of single workers who could be housed in old shacks is no longer typical, so that the cost-differences between immigrant labor on the one hand and indigenous labor or labor-saving rationali-

---

Originally published in *Radical America* 8 (November-December 1974) pp.55-77. Republished with permission.

zation measures on the other are much reduced. In addition—and here we see the connection between the strikes of 1973 and the stopping of immigration—the immigrant workers are no longer willing to put up with the worst forms of exploitation. Strikes against low pay and actions such as rent strikes, house occupations, and demonstrations against bad social conditions have made it clear to the capitalists that, along with the immigrant workers, they have imported a new potential for social conflict. Unlike the German workers, the immigrants have not gone through the stultifying process of fascism, anti-communism, and control through social-democratic parties and union bureaucracies. They are often prepared to take militant action. The bosses fear that the spark may ignite the hitherto passive German proletariat.

The immigration stop, combined with the recession, has already led to a large reduction in the number of immigrant workers since the last year, although an exact figure is not yet available. As in 1966, the bosses are able to export a large proportion of unemployment, thus reducing social conflict at home. At the same time, racist campaigns are used to whip up feelings against immigrants, diverting attention from the real causes of the economic difficulties.

Despite these changes since the completion of the article, immigrant labor will remain a major factor in the German economy for the foreseeable future, and the arguments and hypotheses outlined below maintain their validity.

S.C. and G.K., October 1974

## Introduction

Since the middle of the sixties, West German capitalism has been running into increasing difficulties, which has reduced willingness to make economic concessions to the working class. The result has been a gradual move away from the apathy characteristic of many workers during the period of the "economic miracle" (1949-65), and an increase in class conflict. A peak in this development was the unofficial strike movement in 1973. A new factor in this movement was the leading role played by immigrant workers in many strikes. In some cases they led the strikes or even struck alone, in others they acted as catalyst in factories where German workers were also militant.

The militancy of the immigrant workers creates fresh and pressing problems for the trade union leadership. In order to understand these and the measures which result from them, two questions must first be answered:

1. What function does the employment of immigrant workers have for West German capitalism and what changes have there been in this function over the last fifteen years?
2. What is the general function of the trade unions in West German capitalism and what is their specific function in regard to the immigrant section of the proletariat?

After this we will describe the actual policy of the unions since the beginning of the recruitment of the foreign labor and then discuss possible reactions of immigrant workers towards trade union policy.

## The Function of Immigrant Labor in West German Capitalism

The employment and supper-exploitation of underprivileged groups in most capitalist countries—for example, the blacks in the U.S.A. and South Africa, the rural-urban migrants in Italy and Japan, and the immigrant workers in almost all Western European countries—has two main functions:

1. The unemployed masses form an industrial reserve army which puts pressure on wages, thus helping to keep the profit rate high.
2. The working class is split according to race, nationality or area of origin.[1]

The underprivileged position of one section of the working class is complemented by the somewhat better position of another section. Like the whites in the U.S.A. and South Africa, the indigenous workers in Western Europe tend to have certain privileges, better working conditions and higher pay. The mass media, the official propaganda apparatus and the educational system deepen the split in the working class by spreading nationalism and racism in order to gain the collaboration of the privileged section of the working class in oppressing the other. The result is the creation of a "labor aristocracy" prepared to defend its apparent economic and social security by betraying its real class interests. This weakens the labor movement. Discriminatory legislation (in Germany the Ausländergesetz—Foreigners Law—of 1965; in Britain the 1971 Immigration Act) denies vital civil and political rights to the already underprivileged section of the working class, which deepens the split.

The use of an external or foreign reserve army became necessary for the capitalists in West Germany later than in other countries. Up until 1961 three other labor sources were available to put pressure on wages, keeping up profits and allowing the long-lasting export-led boom known as the "economic miracle." These were: the large number of unemployed created by the collapse of the Nazi war economy in 1945, the seven million expellees in the territories lost to Poland, the Soviet Union and Czechoslovakia at the end of the war, and three million refugees from the German Democratic Republic. The first labor shortages appeared in building and agriculture in the mid-fifties, and the bilateral labor recruitment agreement with Italy—the first of its kind—was made at this time.

The employment of immigrant workers was initially regarded by employers, unions and government as a temporary measure. But by the beginning of the sixties the existing domestic labor reserves had been absorbed, the stream of refugees from East Germany had stopped, and it had become apparent that further internal reserves (rural-urban migrants, no-yet-employed women, could not be mobilized to an appreciable extent. Nationalization and the replacement of relatively labor- intensive methods of increasing production by capital-intensive

30

methods were not in themselves sufficient to maintain the growth and competitiveness of West German industry. Capitalists began to recruit (through an efficient state recruitment system) large numbers of workers from the undeveloped parts of Southern Europe and from Turkey. In this way they were able to prevent rapid wage growth in the unskilled and semi-skilled categories.

By the mid-sixties the employment of immigrant workers had become an essential part of West German economic structure. By 1966 there were 1.3 million immigrant workers (not counting dependents). But the government continued to emphasize that immigration was not a permanent factor for Germany, in order to avoid making the social expenditure—on housing, schools, health facilities—which was already necessary. The employers regarded the immigrant workers as a "mobile labor potential," as Ulrich Freiherr von Gienanth, an official of the German Employers' Association, put it. They could be got rid of quickly in case of economic difficulties. "It would be dangerous to limit this mobility through a large-scale settlement policy," wrote Gienanth in support of the government policy.[2]

The advantages (for the bosses) but also the limitations of this labor market policy became apparent in the 1966-67 recession. The causes of the recession were, on the one hand, the increase in wage levels in the years immediately preceding, on the other, the rising level of international competition. The recruitment of immigrant workers could not hold back wage growth to the same extent as had formerly been the case with the internal labor reserves and the refugees from East Germany. The immigrants were mainly without industrial training and experience, lacked general education, and most could not speak German. Their competition could not hold down the wages of skilled and non-manual workers, who together make up more than half the labor force. The braking effect on the wages of unskilled and semi-skilled workers was not sufficient to prevent considerably growth in the general average wage level at this time. The employers used a recession to control wage-growth and restore "labor discipline." A further advantage for the bosses was that they were able to export a substantial part of the social costs of unemployment. For although the number of immigrant workers sank by 400,000 in only a few months, the number of immigrants receiving unemployment benefits was never more than 29,000. In addition a large-scale propaganda campaign against the immigrants by the bosses and their mass-media led to a considerable increase in hostility towards immigrants at this time. The immigrant workers were used as scapegoats to divert attention from the real causes of the recession.[3]

On the other hand the limitations of the "mobile labor potential" policy also became evident. The number of immigrant workers did not fall below 900,000 although large numbers of Germans became unemployed. It became obvious that immigrants could not always be easily replaced by German workers, because they were concentrated in certain industries (building, engineering, chemicals) and above all in certain socio-economic groups (unskilled and semi-skilled manual).

Qualified German personnel were often unwilling to take such jobs. In addition, the employers frequently sacked older German workers rather than young immigrants who, due to their lack of industrial experience and their need to earn a lot quickly, could often be conned into working their guts out on piece- rates. Moreover, even then a large number of immigrant workers had already brought over their families and become firmly established in a specific area. All in all, it proved impossible to make the immigrant workers bear the full burden of unemployment in the recession.

After the recession the number of immigrants employed rose steeply once again, reaching a peak figure of 2.4 million in 1973. Including dependents, there must be close to four million immigrants in West Germany. Eleven per cent of all employed persons are immigrants, and the quota is far higher among manual workers in industry—20 to 25 per cent. In addition to its political function for the ruling class (division of the workers), immigrant labor has today a double economic function: one section of the immigrant labor force remains a "mobile labor potential" which can be moved from branch to branch or sent home as the interests of capital dictate; another section provides most of the labor in certain industries and occupational categories (those with the worst pay and poorest working conditions). This second group cannot be dismissed easily, as there are not enough German workers willing and able to replace them.

The legal administrative measures of the German authorities reflect the role assigned to immigrant labor. Immigrants' political rights are severely restricted by the Foreigners Law and by new regulations issued since. A special department of the *Vergassungsschutz,* the German equivalent of the F.B.I., watches over immigrants, and it is known that the authorities tolerate the activities of Spanish, Greek, Persian and other secret police and even cooperate with them. Any immigrant who steps out of line is likely to be expelled immediately. A system of varying types of residence permits conferring different rights helps to divide the immigrants among themselves: hard-working, "politically reliable" immigrants get privileges compared with the others. On the other hand, efforts are made to keep part of the immigrant labor mobile, in order to save the social costs which cannot be avoided in the long run in case of permanent settlement. The state government of Bavaria went so far as to introduce a "rotation policy," according to which no immigrant should be allowed to stay more than five years. Such measures are in part a reaction to the growing unwillingness of immigrants to accept the worst social conditions, which has been shown in a wave of rent strikes and squatting in the last few years. A further measure has been the recent increase in the recruitment fee of the state recruitment service: an employer must now pay DM. 1000 (over $250) per worker, instead of DM. 300. This has had little effect, however, since many employers (illegally) pressure the workers into paying the fee back to them.

## The Function of the Trade Unions with Regard to Immigrant Workers

The trade unions of the German Federal Republic have long since become a stabilizing factor in the capitalist system. With its Dusseldorf Program of 1963 the D.G.B. (German Trade Union Federation) accepted the capitalist form of economic growth and made this its own goal. This means that the unions—like the employers—must have an interest in guaranteeing capital accumulation through high profit rate, which means relatively low wages. The unions are therefore compelled to restrain their members from wage demands and industrial action which might endanger the high profit rates.

On the other hand, the unions cannot openly oppose the day-to-day interests of their members. This would lead to a weakening of the union's basis through loss of membership, so that it would no longer be capable of carrying out collective bargaining or industrial action. Such weak unions do not even serve the interests of the bosses: the ideology of "social partnership" requires unions at least strong enough to canalize and restrict the demands of the workers.[4] If the unions become too weak the probable result is spontaneous mass movements outside their control, which may eventually lead to revolutionary forms of organization. Thus even unions which support the capitalist system cannot afford to entirely ignore the demands of their members.

The unions therefore work in the following way: they represent the interests and demands of the members to a limited extent. In case of disputes they take over the leadership and then take the steam out of the movement through long- drawn-out negotiations and formalized procedures which eventually only get out of the bosses what these can afford to pay without endangering profits.[5] The increasing difficulties of West German capitalism in recent years make this double task of the unions more and more arduous. The capitalists attempt increasingly to move away from a free labor market in order to allow long-term planning of wage costs. Incomes policy in Germany takes the guise of voluntary "concerted action" and "stability policy" in which the unions participate. This makes it increasingly difficult for the unions to even appear to represent their members. The result is an increasing tendency towards spontaneous movements—notably the waves of unofficial strikes in 1969 and 1973—which question the policies and structures of the unions.

What does this dual function of the unions mean for their policy towards immigrant workers? In so far as the recruitment of immigrant workers serves capitalist growth, it is supported by the unions. However, as the presence of immigrant workers tends to harm the interests of German workers by keeping down wages, the union must try to alleviate these effects. They do this by demanding equal pay for immigrant workers and by calling for measures to aid social integration from the government. Integration and control of the immigrant workers also fits in with the interests of the union leadership, who fear that immigrants may become more militant than German workers. Through measures like the setting up of advisory services and the publication of information in foreign languages, it is hoped to get the immigrants into the unions and to reduce their potential for independent unofficial action.[6]

The unions face a dilemma: on the one hand they must try to prevent immigrants being used to put pressure on wages, on the other hand labor immigration is profitable for capital just because it keeps wages down and splits the working class. If the unions carry out their system-stabilizing task of limiting wage demands, then they must act against the demand of the members, who want this downward pressure on wages eliminated. The unions try to solve this contradiction by trying to convince the German and immigrant workers with resounding phrases that their interests are being looked after, while at the same time pursuing a policy of disciplining the immigrant workers. The dialectical repressive function of the unions is shown in their policy towards immigrant workers yet again: the unions can only support the capitalist system if they are able to appear not as oppressors but as mediators, on the one hand between labor and capital, on the other between German and immigrant workers. The unions tend to lose their function to the extent that the workers come to understand it. But if the unions are no longer capable of fulfilling their integrative mediation function, then the workers are compelled to fight—either spontaneously or in new organizations—against the now evident power of capital.

*Union Policies Towards Immigrant Workers*

The contradictory aims of the unions are justified in the following way by the Federal Executive Committee of the D.G.B.:

> In order to surmount existing labor market bottle-necks, the D.G.B. and its member unions agreed in principle in 1955 to the employment of foreign employees. They saw in this a necessary contribution to safeguarding full employment in an expanding economy and at the same time a practical step of social and trade union solidarity. In order to prevent foreign employees being used as wage-cutters, the D.G.B. demanded right from the outset that recruitment abroad should not be carried out directly by the employers but rather in the framework of definite labor market policy through the Federal Labor Office. The Federal Government agreed to this. In every case the principle of equality with German employees in wages, labor and social rights is to be applied.[7]

In fact, the legal recruitment monopoly of the Federal Labor Office does not prevent illegal recruitment by so-called "slave dealers," nor does formal equality prevent de facto discrimination against immigrants at work. Even real wage equality would not prevent the foreign reserve army from putting pressure on wages, as the expended labor in itself tends to keep wages down. As to the working and living conditions of immigrants, it is therefore not so much what the unions have achieved in terms of formal guarantees that counts, but rather that they have to fight actual discrimination and to achieve concrete improvements.

The unions have protested against the more spectacular examples of "slice-dealing." They have demanded better working conditions and safety regulations, they have complained about the bad housing conditions and restricted educational opportunities of the immigrants, they have demanded reforms in the Foreigners Law to ease family reunification and to give "well-behaved" immigrants, the right to settle in West Germany. But all these campaigns have taken the form of verbal demands and appeals to the humanity of the exploiters. The unions have not led a real struggle for change. Above all, they have never used their main weapon, the strike, to force the bosses to improve immigrant workers' conditions. They have done little more for the immigrant workers than to play the role of a social fire brigade, which appears where the system show its worst aspects. They act like a charitable organization which alleviates the worst effects of the capitalist market economy and in doing so helps to safeguard the system as a whole.

The analogy to a charitable organization is not coincidental. In West Germany social work with immigrants has been delegated by the government to voluntary organizations, mainly religious ones. Like these, the unions have set up advisory offices, which are partly financed by the government. Here immigrants can get advice on problems concerning work, family housing, law and so on. The unions treat the other social services as competitors, as the following quotation from a report of the Metal Workers Union (I.G.M.) shows:

> Where these social services detect a weakness in the work of the trade union organization, where there are no shop stewards for the foreign colleagues or where the stewards remain passive or do not receive adequate support, particularly where the works council does not take action in the case of complaints from foreign employees, there the social services take special satisfaction in outdoing the union in its very own field—particularly in the eyes of the public and the foreign employees. [8]

In examining the relationship of the unions to the immigrant worker, one cannot limit oneself to describing special union social services for them. Much more important is the participation of the immigrant workers in the normal life of the union, as shown by membership and the holding of union offices. At the beginning of 1971 the six main immigrant nationalities (Yugoslavs, Turks, Italians, Greeks, Spaniards, Portuguese) had an average membership rate of 22.4 per cent. The Turks and Spaniards had the highest membership rate (27 per cent), the Yugoslavs (17 per cent) and the Portuguese (15 per cent). The membership rate varies considerably from industry to industry. The Chemical Workers Union (I.G. Chemie) has organized 43 per cent of all immigrants working in its sector. [9] Nearly one third of all immigrant workers in the metal industry are members of the Metal Workers Union (I.G. Metall), indicating a membership rate only slightly below that of German workers. This is all the more astonishing when one take into account that most immigrants are of rural origin and that trade union membership may lead to repressive measures by the reactionary governments in the countries of origin upon return.

But the immigrant workers are considerably unrepresented among trade union office holder. In 1973 only 5,633 foreign workers were elected as shop stewards of the Metal Workers Union—4.7 per cent of all stewards elected.[10] This is an improvement compared with 1970, when only 2.4 per cent of all stewards were immigrant workers, but is still low when one considers that about 10 per cent of the union's members are immigrants. On average there is one foreign shop steward for about every forty foreign union members in the metal industry, compared with one German steward for every fifteen German union members.[11] Under-representation is still greater with regard to works councils.[12] Since 1972 foreigners have had equal rights to be elected as works councillors, but they still have to overcome greater difficulties than German colleagues when they wish to represent their compatriots. The Metal Workers Union only puts immigrant with a good knowledge of German on its candidates lists, which excludes many able and militant immigrants. Unions often give the best places on the lists (which is decisive due to the system of proportional representation) to workers who have been in the factory longest. This practice is disadvantageous to immigrants, and was one factor in the conflict between immigrant workers and the works council at Ford of Cologne during the strike in August 1973 (which will be described below). A Turkish union member standing for election in the 1972 works council elections was assigned, despite his popularity, a very low place on the candidates list. When the local union leadership refused to give him a better place he stood for election on an independent list and was elected with a very large number of votes. Against this, the works council majority refused to apply for him to be released from work to carry out his works council duties, accusing hum of anti-union behavior.[13]

Altogether, 1,445 immigrants were elected as works councillors in the metal industry in 1972; that makes 2.2 per cent of the total elected. This compares with an immigrant share in the labor force in the factories concerned of 14.2 per cent.[14] It seems likely that immigrant workers are even more under-represented in other industries, with the possible exception of chemicals. The degree of under-representation varies from nationality to nationality and is probably greatest for the Turks, the largest and on average most recently arrived group of immigrants. The Greeks, Italians and Spaniards are somewhat better represented, though still much worse than Germans.

If the unions seriously want strong immigrant participation, then they need to take measures to improve the representation of immigrants in trade union offices and works councils. The Ford strike showed how great the gulf between the unions and the works council on the one hand and immigrant workers on the other has become in some cases: here the Turkish workers refused to negotiate with the employers if the works council took park in the meetings. They regarded the works council as a tool of the bosses which had sold them out. The under-representation of immigrants in union representative functions leads to the supposition that the union leadership wants only the passive membership of the immigrants, but is basically concerned above all with the interests of the German workers.

The most important criterion for the policy of the unions towards immigrant workers is their behavior in actual industrial conflicts in which immigrants are involved. Here it is only possible to mention a few cases, which however may be regarded as fairly typical for the behavior of the unions.[15] There are three basic types of conflicts, which require varying responses from the unions.

Firstly there are general conflicts between labor and capital, which are not necessarily carried out within the factory. The most important case was the anti-immigrant campaign between 1964 and 1966.[16] This was a large scale propaganda campaign of the bosses, who, through their mass media,tried to create hostility towards immigrants and to use it to fight against the trade union demand for shorter working hours. The campaign started with the speech of the then Federal Chancellor Erhard in May 1964. He called upon German workers to work longer so that the immigrants could be sent home. The peak of the agitation was the headline in the mass-circulation *Bildzeitung* of March 31, 1966, which asked provocatively: "Do foreign workers work harder than German workers?" The climate of hostility towards immigrants was such that the headline led to a series of fights and unofficial strikes. The unions tried to counter the campaign through articles in the trade union press and leaflets distributed in factories. In some cases meetings were held to discuss the problems of the employment of immigrant workers. But no decisive steps were taken to fight against the anti-immigrant propaganda. Offensive measures like strikes or overtime bans were never even considered. The moral appeals for international solidarity were not successful in reducing hostility towards immigrants, as a series of opinion polls taken at this time show.[17] As the unions basically support the capitalist system, they were unable to show how exploitation of the industrial reserve army and the use of propaganda to divide up the workers is an intrinsic part of capitalism that can only be combatted by fighting the system as a whole. The moral appeals could have no effect on the workers, who know perfectly well that the bosses recruit immigrants to keep down wages and raise profits. In retrospect the anti-immigrant campaign of 1964-66 can be seen as the ideological preparation for the 1966-67 recession, during which the unions were just as helpless in preventing the splitting of the class and in defending immigrants' rights as they had been during the preparatory phase.

Secondly, there are industrial conflicts in which unions carry out official action to secure higher wages. In such cases, the West German employers often try to weaken the workers' front through special forms of repression against the immigrants. For example, during the rubber workers' strike in the State of Hessen in November 1967, the management tried to break the strike by threatening to expel the immigrants from the works' hostels if they did not resume work immediately. At the same time they distributed a leaflet to German workers, blaming the strike on the immigrants, whom they described as "a drunken Mediterranean horde." In this case the Chemical Workers Union was able to take measures which successfully countered these attempts to split the workers, and the strike was won.[18] Frequently, immigrants who strike are threatened by the bosses with deportation, and the authorities collaborate in such measures. However, the authors know of no industrial dispute in which immigrant workers have allowed themselves to be used as scabs. On the contrary, the solidarity shown in the behavior of the immigrants often leads to the removal of prejudices during industrial disputes.[19]

Thirdly, there are industrial disputes in which immigrant workers fight against special forms of discrimination. Such struggles, which aim at combatting the oppression of immigrants, seldom receive support from the unions and German workers, and tend more and more to take the form of unofficial strikes. Examples are the strikes at Hella in Lippstadt in September 1969 and July 1973, and at Kharmann, Ford, and Pierburg in 1973.

The Hella car components factory in Lippstadt has the distinction of being one of the few factories which played a prominent part in the strike movements of both 1969 and 1973. In both cases, immigrant workers took the lead. In 1969, 95 per cent of the workers in the northern branch works were immigrants, manly Spanish and Italian women, graded as semi-skilled. They were paid much less than the German workers in the main works, who were for the most part skilled. The immigrants had had to sign contracts, which they could not properly understand, in their countries of origin. Wage discrimination was the original issue in the strike. In addition, demands were made concerning Christmas bonuses, which the management cut when workers had been off sick, and the length of holidays. The German workers gave the strike some verbal support but did not join in. The Metal Workers Union tried to get the immigrants back to work: the claims were justified, said the officials, but the methods of an unofficial strike was not permissible. The management called in the police and the consuls of the countries of origin. The immigrant women found themselves unable to continue against this united front; they returned to work without achieving their demands.

The behavior of management and union had not changed in 1973 at Hella. The German workers were given an "inflation-bonus" of 15 pfenning per hour, while the immigrants got nothing. In this way the bosses successfully split the workers, for the Germans took no part in the subsequent strike of the immigrant workers. The Metal Workers Union once again opposed the strike. The bosses called in the police and the consuls. But this time the immigrant workers had elected a militant strike committee which led the struggle. Their unity resulted in victory: an increase of 40 pfenning per hour for the lower wage group and 30 pfenning per hour for the upper one.[20]

The strike at the Ford factory in Cologne in August 1973 was to date the most important expression of workers' resistance against their super-exploitation. It also showed most clearly the gulf between the union apparatus and the immigrant workers. Ford has 34,000 employees of whom more than half are immigrants, the largest group being the 14,000 Turks. The Germans have mainly skilled or supervisory posts, as have some of the Italians. THe semi-skilled work, particularly the extremely arduous and intensive assembly work on the production-line, is carried out almost entirely by Turks. Management has used the special situation of the Turks—their poverty and rural origins, the long waiting lists (about a million Turks have applied for work in Germany) at the German recruitment centers—to raise the speed of production at an unbearable level. The shop stewards and works councillors, nearly all skilled German workers, who do not understand the problems of the Turks, have done nothing to prevent this and have therefore lost the trust of the immigrants. As early as 1964, a survey carried out on behalf of the Metal Workers Union showed how great the gap between German and immigrant workers had become,[21] but no effective measures were taken to change the situation. The works council elections of 1972, already mentioned above, were another danger sign which was ignored.

The strike started when 300 Turkish workers were fired because they overstayed their holidays. The 20-day annual holiday is far too short for those who have to travel for seven or eight days to reach their families in Anatolia. The sacked workers were not replaced, making the pace of work even greater for those who remained. The result was a spontaneous strike in one department, which quickly spread throughout the works. A strike committee was elected and demands were made which at first united immigrant and German workers: a raise a 1 DM, per hour for all workers, reinstatement of the sacked workers, six weeks paid holiday, reduction of production-line and machine speeds, more workers on the line and the machines. This immigrant-led strike at a major industrial plant terrified the German bosses, and they used all the weapons at their command to break it. Together they condemned the strike, which, they alleged, was led by foreign communist agitators. Large police forces were made ready. The *Bildzeitung* mobilized nationalist feelings with headlines about "Turkish Terror at Ford." The works council did everything possible to undermine the unity of the workers. By making concessions on pay, which was the main issue for the German workers, the management was able to divide them from the Turks. This made possible an attack on the strike leadership by supervisory staff assisted by disguised policemen. The leaders were arrested and the demoralized Turks were forced back to work by threats of dismissal and deportation. The *Bildzeitung* celebrated the event with the headline "German workers liberate their factory" (as if the factory belonged to the workers!) while the Ford management praised the works councillors for their help and their "physical courage" in fighting against the workers. Ford is an extreme example of how German trade unionists have become tools of management against the immigrants, who now have to fight not only against the bosses and against the police, but also against their own "representatives."

An important factor in the Ford strike, as in other strikes in 1973, was that the immigrants were fighting not only for higher pay but also for better working conditions, in particular for a reduction in the health-destroying work-pace on production lines and in piece-work. Traditionally, the West Germans have not struggled for such demands. Rather they have become "wage-machines" concerned only with raising pay-rates through national negotiations. In the collective bargaining and official strike in Baden-Wurtemberg in the autumn of 1973, immediately following the unofficial movement, the Metal Workers Union for the first time raised demands concerning working conditions.

To sum up, it may be said that the unions seldom take account of the special needs and interests of immigrant workers, and that the immigrants often do not feel that the unions represent them. In many cases they see the local representatives of the unions as tools of the bosses. Such problems do not concern the immigrants alone. Most shop stewards and works councillors are German skilled workers or even foremen.[22] They tend first and foremost to represent the interests of the group from which they come. It is not just the immigrant workers whose interests are neglected—the same applies to all unskilled and semi-skilled workers. Apart from immigrants, the largest group in these categories are women workers who in West Germany, as elsewhere, are considerably underpaid. This explains why the unions generally make demands for a percentage rise in wages, which corresponds to the interests of better-paid workers by maintaining differentials, but until the strikes of 1973 did nothing against piece-work and inhuman working conditions.

### Trade Union Organization or Self-Organization for the Immigrant Workers

In the struggles of 1973 the unions showed themselves on the whole to be incapable of fighting for the special interests of the unskilled and semi-skilled workers, in particular of the immigrant workers. This applies not only to the national leadership but also to the union representatives at the factory level. At present the unions seem unable to fulfill either of their contradictory functions adequately: they neither represent the whole of the working class, nor do they serve the interests of the bourgeoisie effectively, for they no longer have the workers under control.

It is not yet evident how the unions will behave in this situation. One the one hand, they are likely to take further special measures to encourage the "social integration" of the immigrants and to increase their loyalty to the unions. Advisory services, language courses and special training facilities for immigrant union members might increase the unions' control over immigrant workers. On the other hand an increased witch-hunt for "foreign agitators" is probable. This would mean, however, that union officials might in some cases become agents of the foreign police. The hysterical reaction of many officials to the Ford strike indicates that such a development is not impossible.

Active and class-conscious unionists cannot support such strategies. It must be their task to increase the number of immigrant shop stewards and works councillors, with the aim of bringing them into the struggle for returning the unions to their original aim: that is, to represent the workers in the fight against capitalist exploitation. The unions must be made to move away from their policy of collective bargaining on a national or state level and instead to make demands which concern the immediate, concrete, local interests of the various groups of workers—demands concerning not only wages but also the humanization of working conditions. But a change in union policy in this direction is hardly to be expected and will certainly not come from the present leadership, for it would mean rejecting the stabilizing role which the unions have come to have for the capitalist system.

If the unions do not take such steps to become truly representative of immigrant workers' interests, then the question of the self-organization of the immigrants will become pressing. Self-organization means that the spontaneous and temporary coalitions of immigrant workers, which come into being in strikes when the unions fail to support the immigrants, could gradually become permanent organizations, representing immigrant workers at first locally, then regionally, and even for the whole country. but the development of "national" or multinational" organization carries with it the danger of a repetition of the tragic error of the R.G.O. (Revoluationare Gewerkschaftsopposition—revolutionary trade union opposition) policy carried out by the German Communist Party at the beginning of the thirties. By splitting up the workers and making the militants easily identifiable, this policy did much to help the bosses and Nazis in destroying the labor movement in 1933. Separate unions for immigrants and Germans would mean institutionalizing the split in the working class, and would serve the interests of the employers. A joint struggle of immigrants and Germans would become very difficult.

But union officials who see an R.G.O. under the bed every time attempts are made to improve the trade union representation of immigrant workers are needlessly alienating the immigrants. In the last analysis, the decision whether to form separate organizations or not can only be taken by the immigrant workers themselves. But such decisions are affected strongly by union policy. If unions are unable to represent discriminated groups, if union officials become tools of the bosses and participate in discriminatory policies, then independent organizations cannot be avoided in the long run. In the U.S.A. and South Africa, where the established unions have in part become organs of racism, the formation of independent black organizations was a necessary and correct step. Things are not (yet) so bad in West Germany: few union officials consciously serve the interests of capital; most oppose the discrimination and super- exploitation of immigrant workers, at least verbally. But if this verbal opposition is not in the near future transformed into effective policies, then there can be little doubt that a section of the immigrant workers will look for new forms of organizations.

# Notes

1. For a fuller treatment of these problems see: Stephen Castles and Godula Kosack, "The Function of Labor Immigration in Western European Capitalism." *New Left Review* (73, July 1972).
2. Gienanth, "So schnell geht es nicht," in *Der Arbeit-Geber* (March 20, 1966).
3. For further details see: Stephen Castles and Godula Kosack, *Immigrant Workers and Class Structure in Western Europe* (London, 1973) 167ff and 430ff.
4. The example of the Swiss unions shows what happens when unions all too obviously collaborate with the bosses and betray the interests of the workers. There have been hardly any official strikes in Switzerland since 1937, when the unions made an "industrial peace" agreement with the bosses. The result is that the unions are rapidly losing membership. In particular the unions, due to their nationalistic policies, have been unable to organize most immigrant workers. Today these unions are being increasingly ignored, even by the bosses.
5. See Walter Muller-Jentsch, "Entwicklungen und Widerspruche in der westdeutschen Gewerkschaftsbewegung," in *Gewerkschaften und Klassenkamps, Kritishes Jahrbuch '73* (Frankfurt, 1973) 150ff.
6. See the D.G.B. publication: "Die deutschen Gewerkschaften und die ausländischen Arbeitnehmer" (Frankfurt, November 21, 1971) 9-10.
7. D.G.B. publication: "Die deutschen Gewerkschaften und die ausländischen Arbeitnehmer" (Frankfurt, November 21, 1971) 1.
8. Vostand der I.G. Metall, *Beratungsbericht Zu Den Fragen Gewerkschaft und Ausländische Arbeitnehmer* (Frankfurt, February 5, 1970) 13.
9. Ernest Piehl, "Gewerkschaften und ausländische Arbeiter," in *Gerwerkschaftsspiefel*, No. 1 (1972) 19ff.
10. I.G. Metall, *Schnell information Uber Das Ergebnis Der Vertrauensleutewahlen 1973*. Vertrauensleute are roughly comparable with shop stewards and are elected every three years for a whole industry at once.
11. These figures indicate the degree of representation of immigrants,but do not mean that shop stewards are elected only by specific national groups. Stewards, like works councillors, are of course elected by the whole work force in a factory or department.
12. Works councils can be elected in every West German enterprise with more than 10 employees. They are elected by all employees (not just union members) and have various social and legal functions as laid down in the Works Constitution law of 1972.
13. According to the size of the enterprise, a certain number of works council members are released from work (on full pay) to carry out their duties. Obviously, those released have far more opportunity of representing their colleagues than those who have to go on working.
14. I.G. Metall, *Ergebnisse Der Betriebsratswahlen 1972*, pp.10, 13.
15. For a fuller discussion see: Castles and Kosack, *Immigrant Workers . . .*, pp. 152ff.
16. See I.G. Metall, *Die Ausländerwelle und Die Gewerkschaften* (Frankfurt, 1966).
17. See for instance: "Institut für angewandte Sozialwissenschaft," *Deutsche und Gastarbeiter* (Bad Godesber, 1966) *Divo* Represantativerhebung February 1966, Divo Pressendienst.
18. F. Dobler, "Der Streik in der hessischen Gummiindustrie im November 1967 uter besonderer Berucksichtigung der 'Dunlop' Hanaux" (Hanau, 1968).
19. See Castles and Kosack, "Immigrant Workers . . ." 13.
20. See *Klassenkampf* (Frankfurt, September 27, 1973); *Kommunistische Volkszeitung* (2, September 12, 1973); *Der Spiegel* (September 3, 1973).
21. Institut für angewandte Sozialwissenschaft, *Arbelter-Vertrauensleute-Gewerkschaft*, (Bad Godesberg, 1964).
22. Rainer Riehl, "Der Aufstand der Angelernten," *Klassenkampf* (October 28, 1973).

# The Social Time-Bomb:
# Education of an Underclass in West Germany

## Introduction

The immigration experienced by all Western European industrial nations since 1945 is generally regarded as having two distinct forms: first, the permanent settlement of black citizens from former colonies in Britain, France and Holland; secondly, the temporary recruitment of "guestworkers" from Mediterranean countries for a limited period of employment in West Germany, Switzerland, France, Sweden, etc. The "guestworkers" were a new form of contract labor, not expected to settle or bring in dependents. Their profitability was enhanced by a supposed lack of need for social investments in housing, schools and the like. But even ten years ago there was evidence that temporary migration was going to turn into permanent settlement—even in countries like Switzerland and West Germany, which were vehemently opposed. Moreover (and this was the main thesis of a study carried out by myself and Godula Kosack at the beginning of the 1970s), the function of both groups of immigrants for the capitalist system was the same: to provide a cheap and flexible source of mainly unskilled labor, during a period of rapid industrial expansion, and to facilitate the creation of economic and social divisions within the working class.[1]

The 1970s indeed witnessed the expected change from temporary migration to settlement. But parallel to this convergence in the two forms of migration a more important change was taking place: the function of immigrant workers for capitalism was changing throughout western Europe. The relatively labor-intensive expansion was at an end; the capital accumulation made possible by the exploitation of immigrant labor (together with other factors) now ushered in a new phase of restructuring of the world economy. The policy of the most advanced sectors of capital was now to export capital (and jobs) to low wage countries, rather than to import labor.[2] This meant a decline in industrial employment in western Europe, which was intensified in the mid-1970s by the decline in growth, starting with the so-called "oil-crisis", and in the late 1970s by the rapid introduction of microprocessors.[3] The reaction throughout western Europe was to stop the import of labor and to start repatriation schemes. But although right-wing parties have demanded the repatriation of all immigrants, this has not been the strategy of big capital nor of the governments concerned. A reduced and stabilised immigrant population still has a vital socio-economic function for them: that of a social buffer at the lowest level of society, absorbing the worst impact of restructuring, and helping to cushion higher strata against it. But immigrants can

Orginally printed in *Race and Class* 21.4 (1980) 369-387. Reprinted with permission.

only have this function if legal, social and economic pressures keep them collectively in an underclass position. This is the task of measures restricting entry, labor market and civil rights. In turn, such discriminatory measures lead to responses from immigrant workers in the form of economic and political struggle. So, throughout western Europe we see a process of class formation before our eyes.

The present article will examine the transition from temporary migration to permanent settlement in West Germany, and then look at one aspect of class formation: the way the education system works to guarantee that second- generation immigrants will remain at the lowest occupational and social levels of society.

### How government policies turned temporary into permanent migration—while claiming the opposite

The migration of workers to West Germany started later than to most other countries, but soon developed into the most rapid and highly-organised movement of labor anywhere in postwar Europe. The number of foreign workers rose from 95,000 in 1956 to 1.3 million in 1966, dipped to 900,000 during the recession of 1966-8, and then shot up to 2.5 million by the summer of 1973. Most workers were recruited in their home countries by branches of the German Federal Labor Office.[4] At first, migration was regarded as a transitory necessity, and government policies were designed to keep it that way, by preventing entry of dependents and severely restricting workers' rights. But by the mid-1960s labor demand was soaring throughout western Europe. Regulations were relaxed to attract foreign workers and to increase their flexibility and mobility. It became easier for a worker to bring dependents to West Germany after a certain period. At the same time, many families found their own way of re-uniting by getting the second partner recruited as a worker and bringing in children as "tourists". By 1971, two million foreign workers had about one million non-working dependents with them. Of course, population structure still showed over-representation of young working males and the rate of activity was 66 per cent, compared with about 40 per cent for Germans. Many migrants still came for a few years only, before returning home to set up a small service enterprise, buy land or build a house. But members of this group often re-emigrated to West Germany after a while, when their business failed. A second time, they were more likely to bring dependents, having lost their illusions about the chances of escaping poverty in the underdeveloped south.

Then, in November 1973, the Federal Government suddenly issued the *Ausländerstopp,* an administrative order banning all further immigration of workers from non-EEC countries.* The explanation given

---

*Free movement of workers within the European Community was laid down by the Treaty of Rome and came into force in 1968. It was not affected by the *Ausländerstopp* of 1973. Free movement of workers has taken two forms: 1) Mobility of highly-skilled workers in all directions in the Community. 2) Movement of unskilled workers from the periphery to the core of the industrial areas. In particular there has been large-scale

for this was the falling demand for labor due to the "oil-crisis". The real underlying reasons (as mentioned above) were the growing trend to export labor-intensive production processes to low-wage countries in the Third World, and the changes in the production process beginning to result from the introduction of microprocessors. Further factors which played a part in West Germany were: the costs and tensions caused by the growing social requirements for foreign workers' families; and fears of political conflicts resulting from the leading part played by foreign workers in the strike wave of the summer of 1973.[5]

During the 1973-5 recession, the number of foreign workers fell by over half a million. Since the *Ausländerstopp* remained in force during the following period of expansion, the employment of foreign workers became stabilised at just under two million (1,869,000 in mid-1978). But the foreign population did not drop, for existing legislation gave more and more of the workers the right to bring in dependents. In terms of numbers, the departing workers were replaced by the wives and children (and sometimes parents) of the workers who remained. The foreign population became stabilised at just below four million (3,981,000 on 30 June 1978).[6] The rate of activity declined to about 50 per cent, and demands for housing, education and social facilities rose accordingly. The *Ausländerstopp* had changed the whole pattern of migration to West Germany. By keeping out new single workers, it accelerated the tendency towards normalisation of family structures. Moreover, many workers who would previously have remained only a few years and then returned to the country of origin decided to remain, for the chance of a second migration in case of failure at home was now blocked. Such workers became long-term settlers and brought in dependents. Altogether, the 1973 *Ausländerstopp* can be compared with the effects of the 1962 Immigration Act in Britain, in making temporary migration permanent without intending to.

Another piece of ill-conceived and discriminatory legislation reinforced this tendency. The SPD-FDP Government's tax reform, which came into force on 1 January 1975, granted considerably increases in child benefits. However, these were not to be paid to foreign workers whose children remained in the country of origin. This group was to receive only the scale of benefits they would be entitled to in those countries—which meant little or nothing. Despite protests from trade unions and foreign workers' organisations, the Government remained firm, hoping to save about DM 1000m per year.[7] The predictable re-

movement of Italian workers to France, Germany and Belgium. However, movement within the Community is much less in volume than movement to the industrial areas of the Community from outside. For instance, less than one-quarter of foreign workers in West Germany are Community nationals. Since the *Ausländerstopp* of 1973, Community nationals have become a more mobile and flexible source of unskilled or semi-skilled labour than non-Community workers. The southern Italians are being increasingly joined by Irish and British workers. The latter include growing numbers of British citizens of Asian origin, who are attracted by the better wages and employment prospects in West Germany. Fear that free movement of labour would lead to a new influx of Turks has been the reason why the West German Government has opposed the admission of Turkey to the European Community.

sult was that many children who had previously been looked after by grandparents in Turkey, Yugoslavia, etc., were now brought to West Germany. Sometimes the grandparents came too.

A third measure compounded the effects of the *Ausländerstopp* and the tax reform: the *Stichtagregelung* laid down that foreign worker's dependents who entered West Germany after the "key date" of 30 November 1974 were not subsequently to be granted a labor permit.[8] This meant that immigrants' children entering after this date would receive compulsory education, but would not be permitted to take up employment upon completing school. The idea was obviously to force the children who had been brought in because of the tax reform to leave the country again when they became adult. But the actual effect was rather different: many of the young people concerned were unable or unwilling to return to their country of origin, and remained in Germany as "non-persons"—entitled neither to work nor social security benefits. The likely results of such a situation are clear: barred from any legitimate ways of earning a living, such youths have no choice but to take illegal (and highly exploitative) employment or resort to crime.

By 1976 it was evident that West Germany's policy towards foreign workers had become a contradictory shambles. What had started off as a carefully organised movement of short-term workers have turned into large-scale family immigration of long-term and probably permanent nature. The measures taken to control the movement had failed, often achieving the opposite of what was intended. The West German economy, after benefiting for fifteen years from the profits made on relatively low-paid workers, whose dependents were abroad, was not faced with the social costs of integrating a large immigrant population. And there was growing fear of social and political tensions if these costs were not met. At the same time, slowing economic growth and increasing international competition made the cutting of public expenditure imperative.

In this situation the Federal Labor Minister in 1976 convened a Commission, representing Federal and L nder governments, unions and employers, with the urgent task of reviewing migration policies. It report, issued in February 1977, started by declaring: "The Federal Republic is not a country of immigration"—despite the obvious fact that it had long since become one. It called for the maintaining of the *Ausländerstopp* and the *Stichtagregelung,* although the "key date" for the latter was to be extended to 31 December 1976. Apart from this it proposed a "dual strategy" consisting of, on the one hand, measures designed to increase the legal, social and economic integration of immigrants, and, on the other, measures designed to encourage them to go back home.[9]

### The structure of the immigrant population

Government migration policies, such as the "dual strategy" mentioned above, are designed to maximise the profitability of foreign workers, while minimising the social costs. Inevitably they are reflected in the composition and structure of the immigrant population, with regard to nationality, sex, age and family size. Hence, as Table 1 shows, the greatest proportion of immigrants come from the most disadvantaged sending countries.

Table 1: **Selected immigrant groups by sex on 30 September 1978**

(thousands)

|  | All immigrants | Turks | Yugoslavs | Italians | Greeks | Spaniards |
|---|---|---|---|---|---|---|
| Male | 2,320 | 693 | 348 | 357 | 163 | 110 |
| Female | 1,662 | 473 | 262 | 215 | 143 | 79 |
| Total | 3,981 | 1,165 | 610 | 573 | 306 | 189 |

*Source: Statistisches Jahrbuch für die Bundesrepublik Deutschland 1979.*

The Turks form by far the largest national group among immigrants in west Germany. Moreover, this group is still increasing, both absolutely and proportionally, while the other national groups have declined slightly in recent years. The Turks now form 29 per cent of the immigrant population, compared with only 26 per cent in 1975.

Table 1 also indicates the persisting imbalance of the sexes: 58 per cent of immigrants are male and 42 per cent female. This applies to all main groups, but is most pronounced for the Italians (62 per cent males), indicating continuing temporary labor migration for these European Community nationals.

An important indication of the trend towards permanent migration is given by statistics on length of stay, which show that more than 60 per cent of immigrants had been in West Germany for over six years in mid-1978. Twenty- six per cent had actually been resident over ten years. This applies to all main immigrant nationalities.[10]

Moreover, as Table 2 shows, the age structure of the immigrant population is a direct result of a policy of organised recruitment. Two

Table 2: **Immigrants by age on 30 September 1978**

|  | Thousands | % |
|---|---|---|
| Under 6 | 393 | 11 |
| 6-9 | 248 | 7 |
| 10-14 | 246 | 7 |
| 15-17 | 121 | 3 |
| 18-20 | 151 | 4 |
| 21-34 | 1,280 | 34 |
| 35-44 | 770 | 21 |
| 45-54 | 347 | 9 |
| 55-54 | 116 | 3 |
| 65 and over | 79 | 2 |

*Source: Statistisches Jahrbuch für die Bundesrepublik Deutschland, 1979.*

features stand out: the predominance of 21 to 45-year-olds (over half the immigrant population) and the large number of 1 to 6-year-olds.

The first feature indicates the economic benefit of recruiting foreign workers—most are in the most productive age group, and pension demands are far away. But of course, this is also the most fertile age group, which is one reason for the large number of those under 6. Besides, most immigrants come from peasant societies, where, for obvious socio-economic reasons, large families are still the norm. The move to an urban industrialised society should in the long run bring the fertility level close to that of the indigenous population. However, this tendency is countered by the repatriation aspect of the "dual strategy" by undercutting any trend towards "integration", and hence keeping immigrants in a permanent state of insecurity, this policy reinforces existing social and cultural patterns, in particular that of regarding a large family as a form of insurance for old age. So immigrant birth rates have remained high in recent years, while German birth rates have fallen dramatically. The children of immigrants* form a growing proportion of the births in inner-city areas, where the immigrants are concentrated. In recent years, one-third of all births in cities like Stuttgart, Frankfurt and Duisburg have been to foreign parents, a situation which has fed the racism and xenophobia which helped create it in the first place.

At present, as Table 2 show, there are 494,000 immigrant children aged 6 to 15, which is the age group subject to compulsory education in West Germany. They make up 5.8 per cent of this age group. But, for all the reasons mentioned above, the foreign proportion of children aged under 6 is far higher—namely 10.8%.[11] These are the children who will be entering compulsory education in the next few years, so that the proportion of children locked into a permanent second-class status is going to almost double.

### Policies on the education of immigrant children

Education policy is the responsibility of the *Länder* governments rather than the Federal Government, which has merely a coordinating role. *Länder* measures have varied considerably. Since the large-scale entry of foreign children was neither anticipated nor officially desired, nothing was done to prepare for it in advance. In the early years it was not even clear whether schooling should be compulsory for them. There was also confusion as to whether the governments of the countries of origin should be permitted to set up national schools—a course much favored by authoritarian regimes such as those of Spain, Greece and Turkey, as a means of political and cultural control. By the late 1960s most of the thirteen *Länder* had made attendance at German schools compulsory, and were beginning to take special measures to tackle the problems of foreign children. But it was not until 1971 that a general policy for the whole Federal Republic was proposed in a Decision of the Standing Conference of Education

---

*Unlike Britain, where children born to immigrants are automatically entitled to British citizenship, children born in West Germany to foreign parents do not gain the right to West German citizenship. Some consequences of this will be discussed below.

Ministers[12] (a consultative body linking Federal and *Länder* authorities). Policy was revised and updated by a new Decision in 1976,[13] although it remained unchanged in most substantial points. The 1976 Decision laid down the following policy aim.

> It is a question of enabling foreign pupils to learn the German language and to obtain German school-leaving certificates, as well as allowing them to keep and improve their knowledge of their mother tongue. At the same time, education measures should contribute to the social integration of the foreign pupils during the duration of their stay in the German Federal Republic. They also assist in the maintenance of their linguistic and cultural identity.[14]

Again we see the "dual strategy" already noted in the case of general policies towards immigrants. School are to help foreign children integrate into West German society, and yet at the same time to prepare them for return to their countries of origin. Accordingly, two main types of special classes have been established:

(a) Preparatory classes, to give intensive language instruction to prepare foreign pupils to join normal school classes.

(b) Classes in the mother tongue, as a compulsory part of school curriculum for foreign pupils, with the aim of maintaining knowledge of the language and culture of the country of origin.

## Immigrant children in education

*Nurseries*

Apart from language, the main problem for immigrant children on commencing school is the extreme difference in the form of socialisation experienced at home and at school. Foreign children share the same difficulties as other working-class children, but have further grave problems of their own. Their background is characterised by two factors: first, pre-industrial forms of production and social organisation, and the associated norms with regard to behavior, sexual roles, family structures and religion; secondly, the crisis and incipient dissolution of these pre-industrial patterns in the face of economic, political and social change (migration itself being one element of this crisis).[15] The socialisation conditions of immigrant children are therefore both contradictory and insecure. The gravity of this problem varies according to duration of stay in West Germany. Foreign children born there are torn between two cultures, but do at least have the chance of learning the language and getting used to the society before starting school. Children who arrive just before starting school (which is common, for parents often leave them with relatives in the country of origin until they reach school age) are faced with a sudden confrontation between two cultures. At the same time they have to learn a new language and get used to a new home situation with parents and siblings they may hardly know. Children who do not arrive until an even later age have the greatest difficulty. Whether they have attended school at home or not, they have great problems in adapting to school in Germany. They are likely to get stuck in preparatory classes with much younger children, and their chances of successfully completing school are very slim.

Nurseries could have a very important function for foreign children born in West Germany or coming at an early age, reducing their educational disadvantage by helping to prepare them for the demands of school. But unfortunately the proportion of immigrant children who go to nurseries is low. On average, 60-80 per cent of 3-6-year-olds attend nurseries in West Germany, but various surveys have shown that the rate of attendance for foreign children is on average only half or less than the rate for German children.[16]

Why do those children who would benefit most from nurseries not attend them? One reason lies in the unfamiliarity of foreign parents with this institution, which is much less widespread in their countries of origin. They mistrust the nurseries and see little use in them. Another factor is the concentration of immigrant families in inner-city areas, where nurseries are least adequate, both in quantity and quality. Moreover, many foreign workers may be unable or unwilling to pay the fees charged by nurseries. Procedures for obtaining free places may be unknown or too complicated for them. Whatever the reason, the fact remains that many immigrant children under 6 are left alone all day. Others are cared for by elder sisters, whose own education is hindered. Some are cared for by unqualified childminders, usually of the same nationality.

Even where immigrant children do attend nurseries, little is done to deal with their special difficulties. There are a few special nurseries—national, bilingual or multi-lingual—which are trying out various strategies for the cultural integration of immigrant children. But the overwhelming majority of immigrant children who attend nurseries go to normal ones, designed to meet the needs of German children.[17] It is extremely rare for the staff of these nurseries to receive any special training on the problems of foreign children, and there are virtually no special educational programmes to deal with the situation. In other words: nurseries do not have much of a "compensatory" effect in dealing with the language and socialisation difficulties of immigrant children. Since the basic dispositions required for success at school are largely provided (or not provided) in pre-school socialisation, most foreign children start compulsory education with a severe handicap.

*Preparatory classes*

Foreign children take the same tests on starting school as German children. If their knowledge of German is thought to be adequate, they start in normal classes. If not, they enter a special preparatory class (*Vorbereitungsklasse*), designed to give intensive instruction in the German language and at the same time to give instruction in the normal German curriculum. Transition to normal schooling is supposed to take place as soon as the pupil is adequately prepared for it—as officially laid down, within two years. The class teacher in preparatory classes is generally a compatriot of the children, while

German language is supposed to be taught by a German.

But the realisation of this policy has met with considerable problems. The transition from preparatory to normal classes is rarely as rapid and smooth as it should be. The causes for this lie both in the cultural problems of migration and in the socio-economic position of foreign children and teachers in West Germany.

As already pointed out, a quarter or more of all school beginners are foreign in many cities. There are districts of industrial towns where the proportion is as high as 80 per cent. Putting children in a one-nationality class may seem an easy solution to many authorities. Sometimes all foreign pupils in a town are collected in one school. This may involve bussing children in from outlying areas. The rationale for this course is that centralisation allows the provision of specialised language and remedial facilities, but frequently this appears to be window dressing. Another explanation is German parents' fear that their children may be at a disadvantage in schools where most pupils are foreign. Inevitably, one-nationality classes and *"Gastarbeiter"* schools tend to become ghettoes, which are hard to leave.

Moreover, the language problems of immigrant children are often far more complex than is realised. Their mother tongue is often not the main language of the country concerned—this applies for instance to Kurds from Turkey, or Slovenians and Macedonians from Yugoslavia. Even where the language is nominally the same, a child's first medium of communication may be a dialect which is very distant from the official language: an Anatolian child may hardly understand Turkish, or a Sicilian child may have great difficult with Italian. So the immigrant child entering a preparatory class may be confronted with a teacher of the same nationality, whose speech he cannot understand. At the same time, immigrant pupils are expected to learn High German from a German teacher (if they are lucky enough to have one). Yet communication with local children may be a much greater priority, and this involves not High German, but a very different local dialect, like Hessisch, Bayrisch or Berlinerisch. Many immigrant children have in effect to cope with four different languages (or even five in the case of Turkish children attending Koran school, where they are taught in Arabic).

Difficulties in preparatory classes are further increased by the wide age range that is often found in them. This is partly because children who are not regarded as suitable for transition to a normal class may remain in the same class for several years. Moreover, pupils newly arrived from abroad are usually put in the first class whatever their age. A 6-year-old Turk born in Frankfurt may find her or himself sitting next to a 9-year-old straight from Anatolia. For instance, an educational social worker in Frankfurt reports working in classes ranging from 6-9 and 7-12-years-old.[18] Even the best teacher is likely to have trouble maintaining discipline and keeping all children interested in such varied classes. This situation hampers learning the German curriculum, so that when a pupil does finally make the transition to a normal class, she or he will probably experience great difficulties.

In fact, many children end up being sent back to preparatory classes.[19]

An important cause of the problems related to the preparatory classes is the insecure and contradictory position of the foreign teachers who teach in them. Since the use of foreign teachers is one of the main planks of West Germany's "dual strategy" towards immigrant children, it is worth looking at the problem in more detail. It is important to note that tens of thousands of teachers have come to West Germany from countries like Turkey, Spain and Greece—not as teachers but as manual workers. They have been forced to migrate by economic need and political persecution.[20] It might be though that members of this group would be the best recruits for teaching their compatriots in German schools, for they are usually fluent in the language and have the knowledge and experience necessary to help in the social integration of immigrant children. But most West German education authorities have been unwilling to employ such teachers. Instead, they have left recruitment to the authorities of the countries of origin. These, in turn, have rejected use of the teachers already in Germany, whose political loyalty is suspect. They have recruited politically reliable teachers in the home country. The amount of special training they receive before coming to Germany is generally negligible, so that many foreign teachers speak little German and have little knowledge of German society upon commencing work. Nor have the West German education authorities provided training facilities to prepare foreign teachers for their specialised and difficult task.

Foreign teachers are paid neither according to their qualifications (which may vary widely), nor according to their actual work as teachers. Employed specifically to teach *Gastarbeiter* children, their contracts are inferior in both pay and conditions to those of German teachers. Unlike German teachers, who are usually granted tenure for life, immigrant teachers have no security of employment whatsoever. They appear to themselves and their pupils as "second- class teachers for second-class pupils."[21] This insecure status certainly hampers the success of foreign teachers in integrating their pupils into the German school system. In fact, an unwitting premium is put on failure to meet declared policy aims: a foreign teacher who successfully prepares his pupils for entry to normal German classes is working himself out of a job. As soon as the number of pupils in his preparatory class falls below twelve, the class may de dissolved and he may be dismissed. This is specifically stated in foreign teachers' contracts of employment.[22] In recent years, the insecurity of foreign teachers has grown. With rising unemployment among German teachers, there is talk of giving them special training to replace foreign teachers in preparatory classes. Whatever, the educational merits of such a course, its present effect is to worsen the already difficult relations between German and foreign teachers.

Statistics on immigrant children's length of schooling in preparatory classes appear to be unobtainable, but there is considerable evidence to indicate that very few children manage the transition after just one year. Many children stay far longer than even two years in preparatory classes. Often the term "preparatory class" is just a euphemism for permanent one-nationality classes—ghettoes within the schools—which prevent rather than facilitate integration into normal classes. As the Frankfurt branch of the Teachers' Union (GEW) has stated:

> From this provisory solution, in the meantime an illegitimate but firmly constituted national school system has become established. This ends for the majority of foreign pupils—namely 65%—without a school-leaving certificate.[23]

Many immigrant pupils spend all of their primary schooling and even some of their secondary-school career in one-nationality classes. Their chance of integrating into normal classes and meeting the requirements of the West German curriculum after this are extremely small. The 1976 Decision tacitly recognised this by legalising permanent one-nationality classes—tacit acceptance of a ghetto situation for immigrant pupils.

*Normal classes*

Clearly, those immigrant children who start their school career in normal classes together with German children, or at least enter such classes after a relatively short period in a preparatory class, have the best chances of educational success. But such children should not be regarded as being without educational problems. They still have language problems as well as all the difficulties mentioned above with regard to contradictory patterns of socialisation. Overcoming these problems requires special attention on the part of their teachers—in other words some sort of "positive discrimination" to compensate for their educational disadvantages. But this is all too seldom available.

Indeed, West German teachers find themselves confronted with a task for which they are ill-equipped. Immigrant children tend to be concentrated in areas where schools are old and overcrowded. In such inner-city areas, foreign pupils may be more than a quarter of the total number in a class, even though there is an official norm restricting the proportion of foreign children in a class to 15 per cent. For instance, the Minister of Education of Lower Saxony stated in 1978 that this *Land* had 203 primary school classes and 96 secondary modern classes with over 20 per cent foreign children.[24] (By contrast there were no grammar or middle school classes with such high proportions of foreign children). Most Germany teachers find it difficult to cope in a large class with several different nationalities.

The widely varying ages of the children transferred from preparatory classes does not help matter. A 10-year-old in a class of 7-year-olds presents enormous problems for the teacher. Bored by the childish subject matter, and ashamed at being put on a level with much younger pupils, the 10-year-old is likely to assert him or herself through aggression and disruption. The whole climate in the class may be damaged by such situations, so that the most liberal teacher may begin to feel hostile towards immigrant pupils. Above all, the teacher simply does not have time to devote himself to the specific problems of each immigrant pupil. There are thirty other pupils who require attention. Moreover, German parent are likely to put pressure on teachers at "parents" evenings', insisting that the teacher should concentrate on their children and not allow them to be held back by too much concern for foreign children in the class.[25]

Very little has been done to prepare teachers for the task of teaching foreign pupils. Until very recently, teachers' training colleges did not provide any special instruction on this topic. Today, there are some courses, but they are still relatively rare. Nor has much been done to provide special teaching material and aids related to immigrant children's situation. There also appears to be little communication between German teachers in normal classes and the foreign teachers in preparatory classes, so that coordination of methods and subject matter rarely occurs—even within one and the same school.

*Classes in the mother tongue*

The evidence given above indicates that the official aim of securing integration and equality of opportunity for immigrant children in the West German education system has not been achieved. Have the authorities been more successful with their other declared aim of preparing children for return home and for re- integration into the school systems of the countries of origin? This is the task of the special classes set up to maintain fluency in the mother tongue as well as to give basic instruction in the history, geography and culture of the home country. Such classes have been set up widely and appear to be available to most children of the main immigrant nationalities. They are financed by the West German authorities, have a duration of up to five hours per week, are compulsory and take place outside normal school hours, putting additional strain on the children, taking up the time required for homework, and so hindering further their normal schooling.

There appears to be little attempt made to coordinate the content of the mother- tongue classes with normal schooling. The foreign teachers generally use the curricula and textbooks of the country concerned, which would appear desirable from the point of view of aiding reintegration later on. On the other hand, it is questionable whether educational contents which are irrelevant to a child's actual situation can lead to successful learning. There is a need for special teaching material relating, for instance, to the situation of being the child of a Turkish worker in West Germany.

It is above all the mother-tongue classes which form a focus for the battle for ideological control of immigrant children. Authoritarian regimes try to select the teachers and influence what they teach. Teachers who are unwilling to conform may have their passports taken away by the Consulate and then be reported to the Aliens' Police, which may lead to deportation. The Demirel Government of the early 1970s forced Turkish teachers to use militarist texts.[26] The Greek Junta employed threats and violence to compel teachers to use textbooks glorifying the fascist dictatorship.[27] Turkish parents are frequently put under official pressure to send their children to Koran schools in addition to the normal mother-tongue classes. Such Koran schools are not only bearers of religion and culture, but also often play a reactionary political role, frequently acting as recruiting bases for the terrorist Grey Wolf organisation. Altogether, it is doubtful whether mother-tongue classes may be regarded as neutral purveyors of national culture. Immigrant trade unionists and political militants may find them a place of bitter conflict, which is carried out at the expense of their children.

There appears to be little hard evidence with regard to the success of the mother-tongue classes in preparing children for re-integration in the country of origin, although there is room for doubt as to their efficacy. What is certain, however, is that they detract from school success within the German system. As more and more children seem likely to remain in West Germany permanently, the role of the mother-tongue classes needs re-examining.

*The consequences*

The inadequacy of official measures concerning the schooling of immigrant children leads to severe educational disadvantage. This takes three basic forms.

First, under-attendance at school. Despite compulsory education many foreign children go to school only for a few years or not at all. To start with, some parents bring in their children illegally as ''tourists'' because they cannot get permission for them to enter as dependents. These children cannot go to school; to do so would mean deportation. For obvious reasons there are no statistics on this group, but there is no doubt of its existence. But many children and young people who are legally resident do not go to school either. If we compare the school attendance of West German and foreign children, we find that 86 per cent of West Germans aged 6 to 18 were at primary or secondary schools. But the figure for foreigners was only 70 per cent.[28] While this cannot be taken as an accurate measure of under-attendance, because of the different age-structures of the German and foreign populations, it certainly does indicate educational underprivilege.

Secondly, under-representation in the upper levels of selective education. West Germany still has a tripartite system (apart from a few experimental comprehensives). In mid-1978 4.4 per cent of all pupils at West German primary and secondary schools were foreigners. Their share was 6 per cent in primary and secondary modern schools (*Hauptschule*), but only 1.4 per cent in middle schools (*Realschule*) and 1.5 per cent in grammar schools (*Gymnasium*).[29] Children of foreign workers are rarely to be found in higher education, and are also very considerably under-represented in all types of occupational training. Where they do attend occupational training establishments, it is usually the general type (*Berufsschule*), which provides general instruction not leading to a useful qualification.[30]

Thirdly, underachievement at school. Immigrant pupils are severely hampered by socialisation and language problems. The preparatory classes fail to compensate for this and do not even permit pupils to keep up with curricula requirement. Immigrant pupils are general years behind their age-standard when (and if) they are transferred to normal classes. If they leave school at 15 they lose several years of schooling. It is possible to apply to stay on longer, but many immigrant parents do not know of this possibility or are unable to make use of it for economic reasons. So not only do most young immigrants not manage to get into grammar or middle schools (the majority do not even reach the leaving standards of the secondary modern school), but it is officially admitted that two-thirds of immigrant school leavers do not obtain the school-leaving certificate of the secondary modern (equivalent to British CSE).[31]

On the whole, it is doubtful whether West German schools provide most immigrants either with useful knowledge or with formal qualifications likely to lead to success in the occupational system. To many immigrants, this type of schooling appears to be of little value. So, many children attend sporadically or not al all. Teenage girls are kept at home to look after younger siblings, and boys are sent out to work long before school-leaving age—illegally and at exploitative wages. Even those who attend regularly are unlikely to obtain a school-leaving certificate. Since this is the minimum requirement for any sort of occupational training or skilled work, most second-generation immigrants are condemned to a life of insecure unskilled labor alternating with unemployment. No wonder that schooling for immigrant workers' children has been widely characterised as "education for bilingual illiteracy".[32]

### The social time-bomb

In recent years, journalists and social workers in West Germany have started referring to second-generation immigrants as the "social time-bomb". This term is mainly used with regard to the *Stichtagregelung* (see page 6? above) which denies a labor permit to young people who entered West Germany after 30 November 1974 as dependents. Barred from legal employment, it was obvious that this group was compelled to resort to illegal work or crime to exist. The spectra of muggings and disorder conjured up by the press caused the Government to move the *Stichtag* (key date) to 31 December 1976. At the time of writing there is much discussion in official circles of removing the *Stichtag* altogether. Will the abolition of the *Stichtag* defuse the "social time-bomb"?

The answer to this question must be "no", for the *Stichtag* is merely one of a series of discriminatory policies which determine the position of second- generation immigrants. This article has concentrated on education, describing the failure of the official "dual strategy", which claims to give immigrant pupils equality of opportunity in the West German education system, while at the same time preparing them for repatriation. Why has this policy failed? The ostensible reason is its inherent contradiction, which puts an unbearable strain on both pupils and teachers, combined with insufficient resources of finance, person-power training and research. But to grasp the underlying reason one must ask: does the West German ruling class really want to grant equality of opportunity to second-generation immigrants? Catastrophic underachievement in education serves the interests of employers and government because it helps keep second-generation immigrants in the lowest stratum of the working class: the stratum of unskilled and unqualified workers, who are going to bear the brunt of the restructuring of the capitalist economy in the coming decades.

The role played by the education system in the formation of a new underclass corresponds with the other main aspects of immigrant workers' socio-economic position in West Germany (which is in turn comparable with the position of immigrants in other western European countries). To get a complete picture of the current process of class formation we would have to examine:

1. The labor market, which immigrant workers have entered at the lowest level. Lack of education and training, as well as discrimination have kept them there. Now that employment and training opportunities are tending to contract, immigrants find their prospects deteriorating. Low occupational status is both a cause of poor educational performance of the next generation, and a result of educational disadvantage in the past.

2. The housing and social situation of the immigrant population. It is necessary to examine the formation of national or multinational communities in inner-city and other areas and the social and economic relationships which develop in them. This includes the question of differentiation of sub-classes and their interaction with the general class system of West Germany. One tendency appears to be the development of an immigrant petit-bourgeoisie, which has the function of providing services (like the retail of national foods) but is also frequently parasitical and exploitive (landlords and labor-only sub- contractors).

3. The triple oppression implicit in the role of the working-class women migrant. This is particularly pronounced in the case of Turkish women. The question of the function of traditional sex roles in the formation of immigrant communities needs consideration, as do changes in these roles through work, education and interaction with modern western European patterns.

4. The development of new types of culture. A Turk in West Germany should not be regarded as someone with either a (partial) Turkish or a (partial) German culture. New types of culture are evolving through migration, and these cannot be regarded as a mere sum of national cultures. There is talk of a general *"Gastarbeiterkultur"* in West Germany, but the concept of specific national-group cultures of migration seems more useful.

5. Policies with regard to residence and nationality. The present legal restrictions on immigrant workers are designed to guarantee maximum control and prevent any collective action against an under-class situation. This applies even to foreign workers' children born in West Germany. They have no right to West German citizenship, and are subject to all restrictions on labor market and civil rights. It is extremely difficult for immigrants to obtain naturalisation, or even permits guaranteeing long-term security of residence. Discriminatory labor market legislation helps keep immigrants in low status jobs, and the fear of deportation hangs over their heads, restricting militancy and causing permanent insecurity. Unemployment or a minor criminal offence are sufficient grounds for expulsion from the country—a particularly appalling threat for second-generation immigrants, who may have no links at all with their parents' country of origin.

6. The general nature of the relationship between the industrial core areas of European capitalism, and the peripheral Mediterranean areas. German capitalists have long regarded southern and southeaster Europe as suppliers of cheap labor and raw materials and as consumers of industrial products. The form of the relationship has changed over the last century, the import of labor being its particular characteristic in the 1960s. This particular form is now in turn being superseded by new relationships, which will have important effects both on the immigrant population in West Germany and on their countries of origin.

So education is only part, albeit an important one, in the current process of class formation in West Germany. It is this creation of a new underclass which is the real "social time-bomb". Cosmetic operations to remove particularly blatant pieces of discrimination (like the *Stichtag*) will not change the basic position of immigrant workers in Wet German society. Of course it would be easy to put a list of measures to paper which would lead to basic changes and could start to bring about real equality for immigrant workers. But this is a pointless exercise, for it ignores the fact that the import of immigrant workers in the 1960s and the creation of a new lower stratum of the working class in the 1970s correspond to the interests of powerful sections of West Germany's ruling class. In the years of rapid labor-intensive expansion of the 1960s, immigrant workers provided a relatively cheap and easily available source of flexible labor. Now that economic growth has slowed, automation has cut labor needs, and capital export to low-wage countries is replacing import of labor, the immigrant population is taking on a new function: it forms a sort of social buffer, cushioning the West German population against the worst effects of the restructuring of the economy. The immigrants bear much of the brunt of change, but educational underachievement appears to provide legitimation of this, while lack of political rights helps to contain protest. Although large-scale immigration has ceased, immigrants remain an important factor in the class structure of West Germany—and of western Europe.

# References

1.  Apart form the sources given, this articles is based on the author's experience in training social workers for work with immigrant children in Frankfurt am Main.
2.  See F. Frobel, J. Heinrichs, O. Kreye, *Die Neue Internationale Arbeitseilung* (The New International Division of Labour), (Reinbek bei Hamburg, Rowolt, 1977), for a very detailed study of the development of "transnational production". An English translation is to be published shortly.
3.  See A. Sivanandan, "Imperialism and disorganic development in the silicon age", in *Race & Class* (Vol. XXI, Autumn 1979).
4.  See Castles and Kosack (1973) 39-43 for a description of migration.
5.  Stephen Castles and Godula Kosack, "How the Trade Unions try to control and integrate immigrant workers in the German Federal Republic", in *Race* (Vol. XV, no. 4, April 1974), and *Radical America* (Vol. 8, no. 6, November-December 1974).
6.  Figures from *Statistisches Jahrbuch für die Bundesrepublik Deutschland, 1979.*
7.  *Handelsblatt* (13 September 1974).
8.  Bundesminister für Arbeit und Sozialordnung, *Vorschläge de Bund-Länder-Kommission zur Fortentwicklung einer umfassenden Konzeption der Ausländer-berschäftigungspolitik* (Bonn, 1977).
9.  Ibid.
10. *Statistisches Jahrbuch für die bundersrepublik Deutschland, 1979.*
11. Author's calculations based on *Statistisches Jahrbuch für die Bundesrepublik Deutschland, 1979.*
12. Beschluss der Kultusministerkonferenz vom 2.12.71, *Unterricht für Kinder ausländischer Arbeitnehmer.*
13. Beschluss der Kultusministerkonferenz vom 8.4.76, *Neufassung der Vereinbarung "Unterricht für Kinder ausländischer Arbeitnehmer".*
14. Ibid.
15. U. Akpinar, A. López-Blasco, J. Vink, *Pädagogische Arbeit mit ausländischen Kindern und Jugendlichen* (Munich, 1977).
16. Akpinar, et al., opcit., summarise these findings on pp. 38-9.
17. This applies, for instance, to 99 per cent of foreign children attending nurseries in Bavaria, according to Akpinar, et al., op. cit., p. 43.
18. Tina Fries quoted in "Auszug aus einem Info des BV Frankfurt-40% aller Grunschulanf nfer Ausl nderkinder", in *Hessische Lehrerzeitung* (January-February 1975).
19. The proportion concerned is as high 40 per cent according to one authority. U. Boos-Nunning and M. Hohmann, "Probleme des Unterrichts in der Grund-und Hauptschule aus der Sicht der Lehrer in Vorbereitungs-und Regelklassen", in M. Hohmann (ed.), *Unterricht mit ausländischen Kindern* (Dusseldorf, 1976).
20. "Verhand Turkischer Lehrer in der Bundesrepublik Deutschland und West Berlin, Offener Brief" (duplicated, 1972).
21. R. Spaeter-Bergamo, "Kinder zweiter Klasse—Lehrer zweiter Klass", in *Hessische Lehrerzeitung* (October 1974).
22. Ibid.
23. "Auszug aus einem Info des BV Frankfurt", see note 18.
24. "Ausländerkinder werden kunftig doppelt gezält", in *Erziehung und Wissenschaft* (No. 1, 1978).
25. I can confirm this from personal experience as a parent with a child at a West German primary school.
26. "Verband Turkischer Lehrer. . .".
27. *Neue Griechische Gemeinde, Gegen Faschismus in der Bildungspolitik* (Frankfurt, 1970).
28. Author's calculations from *Statistisches Jahrbuch für die Bundesrepublik Deutschland, 1979.*
29. *Statistisches Jahrbuch für die Bundesrepublik Deutschland, 1979.*
30. Ibid.
31. Akpinar, 51.
32. Akpinar, 45.

# The Guest-Worker in Western Europe
# An Obituary

The social history of industrialization is the history of labor migration: concentration of capital requires movement of labor. Temporary labor recruitment and contract labor have been significant for centuries, throughout the capitalist world: Chinese labor in Malaya and the Dutch East Indies, Indian "coolies" in the West Indies, and the migrant labor system in Southern Africa are just a few examples. Such systems have often followed on from slavery, and have been seen as preferable in terms of flexibility and controllability. Nineteenth century industrialization in Europe led to large-scale migrations, both internal rural-urban and international. Most were unorganized, but Germany, France and Switzerland did develop systems of temporary recruitment between 1870 and 1914, making considerable efforts to prevent workers from settling. The Poles who helped build the mines and steelworks of the Ruhr, for instance, were forced to leave the country for a certain period each year, to stop them from getting long-term settlement rights. Nonetheless, settlement did take place, and later policies were aimed at compulsory assimilation, through suppression of the Polish language and culture. The largest and most exploitative temporary labor system was that developed by the Nazis to fuel their war economy (See, Castles and Kosack, 1973, for a summary of pre-1945 European labor migration).

After the second world war, several countries rapidly introduced systems of temporary labor recruitment to speed up reconstruction and to compensate in part for wartime manpower losses (The following account is based on Castles, Booth and Wallace, 1984: Chapter 3, which also gives detailed references. Figures quoted without a reference are from this book).

In 1945, the British Government set up the European Voluntary Worker (EVW) scheme, to recruit about 90,000 workers from refuge camps and later from Italy as well. Only single persons were eligible. They were not regarded as permanent residents, and their civil rights were severely restricted. Tied for three years to a job chosen by the Ministry of Labor, they were liable to deportation for misconduct or ill health, and single men and women recruited were rarely allowed to bring dependants with them. British unions took a restrictive view on these EVW's, (Hepple, 1968:49). The system only operated until 1951, mainly because other labor sources were adequate: first British capital's traditional labor reserve in Ireland, and from the fifties onwards the inflow of black workers from the disintegrating Empire. The EVW's comprised only a relatively small share of Britain's postwar immigrants. Today the population of migrant origin (i.e. Common-

Originally published as "The Guest-Worker in Eastern Europe: An Obituary." *International Migration Review* Vol. 20.4 (1986) pp.761-778. Reprinted with permission.

wealth migrants, Irish, foreigners and their children born in Britain) totals over 4 million.

The EVW scheme was a typical guest-worker system, but its relatively small size points to a question, which may be well applied to other countries as well: to what extent does a guest-worker system, which usually entails state control of recruitment, mobility and working conditions, benefit the economy of the receiving country more than spontaneous migration? In the latter case, the labor market itself often works efficiently to assign migrants to the jobs that are available, and this is likely to meet the needs of employers. However, the weakness of the newcomers in the labor market means that they may end up with exploitative wages and conditions, which is harmful not only to them, but often also to local workers and unions. The extreme case of this is the toleration of clandestine migration (important in the cases of France and the USA). The rightless illegal migrant is the dream-worker for many employers, and the nightmare of the labor movement. Yet generalization is difficult on this issue. The restriction of civil and labor market rights in some guest-worker systems can also have extremely serious implications both for the situation of the migrants, and for the unity and strength of the labor movement.

The Belgian Government started recruiting foreign workers immediately after the second world war, through what was called *contingentensysteem*. Workers were recruited under bilateral agreements with Southern European countries, mainly Italy. Most of them were employed in the coal mines and the iron and steel industry. In 1946, about 60,000 Italians were recruited. Although this was temporary labor migration of the guest-worker type, Belgian regulations were fairly liberal about the entry of family members, and many of the workers stayed on permanently. After 1963, the *contingentensysteem* was abolished, but foreign work-seekers continued to come in of their own accord, as "tourists". Once they had employment, they were "regularized". i.e. granted work and residence permits. In a period of rapid economic growth, such spontaneous labor migration responded rapidly and flexibly to labor needs. Migrants found work in a much wider range of industries and enterprises than before 1963. In this period, the Italians were joined by Spaniards and then by Moroccans and Turks.

In August 1974, the Government decided to stop further entry of workers (except from countries of the European Community). The ban took some time to become fully effective, but by the eighties few new workers were entering Belgium, and immigration balances have, on the whole, been negative (See, SOPEMI, 1984). Entry of dependents did continue after 1976 due to liberal regulations concerning family reunification. The foreign population grew from 453,000 in 1961 (4.9% of the total population) to 716,000 in 1970 (7.2%) and then to 851,000 in 1977 (8.7%). Since then, the foreign population of Belgium has fluctuated around 900,000 with a negative migration balance being compensated for by natural increase to migrant parents. As in most West European countries, children of foreign parents born in Belgium do not automatically obtain citizenship of the host country, although there are fairly liberal naturalization provisions. In recent years, most foreigners obtaining new work permits have been spouses and children of workers, entering the labor market for the first time, rather than new immigrants.

## France

The French Government established an *Office National d'Immigration* (ONI) in 1945 to organize recruitment of foreign workers. Labor migration was seen as a solution to postwar labor shortages, and was expected to be mainly of a temporary character (including seasonal workers for agriculture). However, in view of low birth rates, a certain amount of family settlement was envisaged. Recruitment agreements were made with Southern European countries, and French employers had to make a request to ONI and pay a fee. ONI organized recruitment and travel. There was continuous migration of workers to France from 1945 to 1974. Two million European migrant workers entered France from 1946 to 1970 and they were joined by 690,000 dependants. However, the appearance of a highly organized system of recruitment is misleading. ONI's legal monopoly of recruitment of European workers became more and more of a fiction. The proportion of migrant coming as "clandestines" (on tourist visas or without passports) increased from 26 percent in 1948 to 82 percent in 1968 (Office National d'Immigration, 1968).

This was in part a consequence of increasing competition for labor within Western Europe during the boom period. France started recruiting in Italy, but as the labor needs of Switzerland, Belgium, the Netherlands and the German Federal Republic increased, this source became exhausted. ONI proved incapable of meeting employers' needs, and patterns of spontaneous migration developed, first from Spain and Portugal, later from Yugoslavia and Turkey. Workers from the Iberian countries generally had to come illegally, as the dictatorships of the time were unwilling to facilitate movements. Indeed, many workers came as much for political as for economic reasons. Clandestine workers met employers' needs well. They were a flexible source of labor, and their weak legal status compelled them to accept poor wages and conditions. Once they had jobs, clandestine workers were often regularized by the authorities, which granted them work and residence permits. Unions and welfare organizations called for more control, to prevent exploitation of migrants by "slave dealers" (labor-only sub-contractors), unscrupulous employers and landlords.

ONI was only responsible for migrants from European countries. Citizens of France's colonies and former colonies were able to enter freely until the late sixties. By 1970, there were over 600,000 Algerians in France, as well as 140,000 Moroccans and 90,000 Tunisians. Increasing numbers of black workers were coming in from West Africa and the French West Indies. By now the problems of uncontrolled migration were becoming evident: severe housing shortages, which even led to the growth of shanty-towns (called *bidonvilles*) around

French cities, strains on welfare, education and health facilities, and growing racial tensions, with attacks by French racist groups, particularly against black migrants—in 1973, 32 Algerians were murdered.

In July 1974, influenced by the "oil crisis" and the ban on labor migration to the GFR announced in November 1973, the French Government took measures to stop entry of both workers and their dependants (except for those from countries of the European Community). The ban on entries of dependants proved impossible to enforce, for both legal and practical reasons. The official belief that many migrants would leave, and thus alleviate the strains of the growing recession, proved false: the migrant population of France continued to grow, becoming stabilized at around 4.5 million.*

Only one element of the guest-worker system still remains in France: the recruitment of temporary workers for agriculture. Between 100,000 and 150,000 have been recruited each years since the fifties. The figure for 1983 was 101,857. Ninety-seven percent were employed in agriculture, and 83 percent came from Spain (SOPEMI, 1984:22).

It is evident that an intended temporary labor system has become transformed into a permanent settlement situation. This development—typical for Western Europe—has taken place at a time of considerable economic and social stress, and without foresight or planning. The result is that the social and economic costs have been imposed first on the migrants themselves, who have high rates of unemployment and suffer serious housing problems and other social disabilities; secondly on the most disadvantaged groups of the French working class, who find themselves competing for jobs, housing and social services with the migrants. The powerful "common-sense" reaction is to blame the problems on the migrants, and to call for mass repatriation.

Right-wing groups have found a heaven-sent opportunity for agitation, and racism has become a central political theme. The success of Le Pen and his *Front National* is a grim warning of the consequences of a *laisser-faire* labor market policy, motivated only by capital's short-term needs.

### The Netherlands

Like Britain, the Netherlands had both colonial migrants and guest-workers. Large numbers of "repatriates" entered from the Dutch East Indies (Indonesia) between 1945 and the early sixties. Then there was migration from Surinam and the Netherlands Antilles, initially of students, later of workers. Recruitment of Southern European guest-workers started in response to the labor shortages of the sixties. The Government concluded bilateral recruitment agreements with Italy, Spain, Portugal, Turkey, Greece, Morocco, Yugoslavia and Tunisia between 1960 and 1970. This provided a legal framework for migration,

---

*It should be noted that official figures on the foreign population of France are contradictory, with divergences of several hundred thousand between census figures, and data based on the number of residence permits issued by the Ministry of the Interior. This figure, quoted from SOPEMI, 1984:100, is based on the latter.

although actual recruitment was carried out mainly by the employers.

The Mediterranean workers were regarded as temporary labor, who could be used as a buffer against economic fluctuations. The recession of 1967 demonstrated this function: the number of foreign workers fell by about 7,000, so that a proportion of unemployment was exported to the countries of origin. However, 39,000 migrant workers remained, even though unemployment of Dutch workers rose sharply. Employed in jobs rejected by the Dutch, the migrants had become economically indispensible. When the recession ended, recruitment of foreign workers increased rapidly. Recruitment ceased in 1974, but this time the number of foreign workers did not decline, even though unemployment reached much higher levels than in 1967. From the beginning of the seventies, there had been a trend towards family immigration. Now this became more pronounced: by 1977 there were 105,000 workers from the Mediterranean countries (excluding Italy) in the Netherlands, and they were accompanied by 80,000 dependants. By 1985, it was officially estimated that there were 338,000 persons of Mediterranean ethnic origin in the Netherlands, while the total number of members of ethnic minority groups (a broad category including persons of Surinamese, Antillean, Moluccan origin, refugees and gypsies) was 659,000 (SOPEMI—Netherlands, 1985:16).

Again we have a case of import of temporary labor, which was expected to go away when no longer needed. Developments in the post-1974 recession showed that the migratory process could not easily by reversed. It is to the credit of the Dutch Government that this fact was recognized. In 1979 the Netherlands Scientific Council for Government Policy published a well- researched report, showing that most Mediterranean workers were not likely to return home. They had become permanent settlers and should be recognized as ethnic minorities, within the framework of a general minorities policy (Netherlands Scientific Council for Government Policy, 1979). The Government accepted this advice and gave an outline of its new policy in 1981. The groups mentioned above were categorized as minorities, and measures were announced to secure their full participation in society, through improvements in legal status, housing, social services and labor market situation. Legislation against racism and discrimination was introduced, and foreign residents' political rights improved.

It would be wrong to think that the Netherlands have escaped the social and political tensions connected with the formation of ethnic minorities in a period of crisis. Nor have all the policies been adequately implemented. Rising unemployment and increasing inner-city problems have encouraged the growth of racism, and anti-migrant parties have gained considerable support. However, the recognition of the inevitability of a multi-ethnic society, and the introduction of appropriate policies, is certainly a step forward, especially in comparison with some of the neighboring countries.

## Switzerland

From 1945 to 1974 Switzerland followed a policy of large-scale import of labor. Foreign workers were recruited abroad (mainly in Italy) by employers, but admission and conditions of residence were controlled by the Government, in the framework of a guest-worker system. In the early years, policies were extremely restrictive, as there were fears of an impending economic downturn. The aim was to maintain a rapid turnover of foreign workers, to prevent them from settling. The admission of dependents was kept to a minimum, and workers were granted residence permits that could be withdrawn at any time. Large-scale use was also made of seasonal workers and frontier workers (i.e., workers who enter daily from neighboring countries). However, by the sixties, increasing international competition for labor, together with employers' desire for more stable workforces, led to some liberalization: spouses and children were admitted once a worker had been in Switzerland over three years. Foreign workers could be granted "Establishment Permits" conferring more security and rights to a labor market mobility after ten years (five for certain nationalities). An agreement concluded with Italy in 1964 made it easier to bring in dependants, and also allowed seasonal workers to obtain annual residence permits after five consecutive seasons' work in Switzerland.

The number of foreign workers in Switzerland (including frontier and seasonal workers) rose from 90,000 in 1950 to 435,000 in 1960. Rapid growth continued until the summer of 1964, by which time there were 721,000 foreign workers. Then fears of "overheating" of the economy led to the first measures to cut entries. The number of migrant workers declined slightly, but then increased again to 834,000 in 1970, and finally peaked at 897,000 in 1973. By that time, about a third of the total labor force and about half of all factory workers came from abroad. Foreign population rose correspondingly: from 279,000 in 1950 (6.1% of total population), to 570,000 in 1960 (10.8%) and 983,000 in 1970 (15.8%). The peak figure was 1,065,000 in 1974 (over 16%).*

Severe restrictions were imposed on labor migration from the beginning of the seventies. The number of foreign workers fell to 650,000 in mid-1977, then increased again to 738,000 in August 1981—a level which has been more or less maintained since. If we count only workers considered as residents (holders of Annual and Establishment Permits), foreign employment dropped from 599,000 in 1973 to 500,000 in 1977. After 1980, the number started rising again, to reach 530,000 in 1983. However the number of new workers entering is relatively small (24,000 in 1983) and many are either highly qualified persons, or dependants of workers already in the country. Guest- worker recruitment has virtually stopped, although the system remains intact. The

*It is difficult to relate the foreign labor force to the foreign population statistically in Switzerland, as two categories of workers—frontier workers and seasonal workers—are not counted as belonging to the population. The figures on the foreign labor force given here are the peak August figures and include all categories of workers.

use of seasonal frontier workers—the guest-workers *par excellence*—continues, with 100,000 of the former and 105,000 of the latter in 1983 (SOPEMI, 1984).

Foreign population dropped from its 1974 peak to 884,000 in 1979 and then increased to 926,000 in 1983. As in other countries, stopping labor entries led to stabilization of the immigrant population, with an increasing share of non-economically active dependants. Over three-quarters of foreign residents in Switzerland now hold Establishment Permits—a clear indication of the long-term nature of their stay.

Switzerland is the classic case of the guest-worker system. Migrant workers were recruited to allow rates of growth and profit which would have been unthinkable with a restrictive labor market. It was never intended that they should settle permanently. Yet just because they allowed most Swiss employees to move out of the low-pay and low-status jobs, they became indispensable to the Swiss economy. When foreign labor became scarce in the sixties, the authorities had no choice but to improve migrants' rights regarding labor market mobility, family reunification and long-term stay. Migrants had already started turning into settlers by the time the recession started, and could not be expelled.

The Government has been unwilling to face up to the fact of permanent settlement and to provide the necessary housing and social facilities. Migrants' civil and political rights remain extremely restricted. Naturalization is hard to obtain, migrants' children born in Switzerland have no rights to Swiss citizenship, and deportation is possible for a variety of reasons. The migrant population is marginalized, and this reflects a wide- spread attitude of hostility towards them on the part of many Swiss. Since 1970 there has been a series of referenda calling for enforced repatriation. These have been narrowly defeated, but have generated pressure for restriction of migrants' rights. A move to introduce a slightly more liberal Foreigners Law was defeated by a referendum in June 1982.

### The German Federal Republic

West German employers started importing labor later than those of other countries, partly because postwar recovery did not start until after 1948, partly because there were large internal labor reserves—particularly refugees from the East. The GFR therefore draws on the experience of other European countries, as well as on German historical experience with migrant labor, both before 1914 and within the Nazi war economy. The result was the most highly-organized state recruitment apparatus anywhere in Europe—the pinnacle of the guest-worker system.

The Federal Labor Office (*Bundesanstalt fuer Arbeit*—BfA) set up recruitment offices in the Mediterranean countries. Employers requiring foreign labor had to apply to the BfA and pay a fee. The BfA selected suitable workers, testing their occupational skills, giving them medical examinations and screening police records. The workers were brought in groups to Germany, where employers had to provide accommodation—usually in huts or hostels on the work site. The first bilateral recruitment agreement was made with Italy in 1955. At that time temporary seasonal employment in agriculture and building was envisaged, but soon large numbers of workers were going into industry. Further recruitment agreements were concluded with Spain, Greece, Turkey, Morocco, Portugal, Tunisia and Yugoslavia.

The number of foreign workers in the GFR rose from 95,000 in 1956 to 1.3 million in 1966. Then there was a cutback due to the recession, which lasted until 1968. After that, foreign employment shot up, reaching 2 million by 1970 and 2.6 million by the middle of 1973. With half a million new workers per year, this was the greatest labor migration anywhere in postwar Europe, and was a result of rapid industrial expansion, and a simultaneous shift to methods of mass production, requiring large numbers of new unskilled and semi-skilled workers. Many of the workers recruited in Turkey and elsewhere in this period were women.

Policies were shaped by the view that migrant workers were temporary labor units, which could be recruited, utilized and sent away again as employers required. A complex legal and administrative framework was established to control foreign labor (Castles, 1985). To enter and remain in the GFR, a migrant needed a residence permit and a labor permit. These were granted for restricted periods, and were often valid only for specific jobs and areas. Entry of dependants was discouraged. A worker could lose his or her permit for a variety of reasons, which was likely to lead to deportation. This was seen and used as a means of disciplining the foreign labor force. Just as in the other countries, trends toward family reunification could not be prevented. Often spouses came in as workers, and, once in the country, found ways of getting together. The establishment of families was inevitable. The competition for labor in the sixties, and employers' wish to reduce labor turnover encouraged the authorities to act less restrictively towards family immigration. Foreign labor was beginning to lose its mobility, and social costs (for housing, education, etc.) were rising.

These tendencies became more marked after the sudden ban on entries of non-EC workers in November 1973. Although the number of foreign workers did initially decline—from 2.6 million in 1973 to 1.9 million in 1976—the decline in total foreign population was far smaller—from 4.1 million to 3.9 million in the same period. Clearly, family reunification was accelerating, and, in addition, large numbers of children were being born to foreign parents in the GFR. Family reunification reached new levels in the late seventies, as the most recently arrived and largest group—the Turks—also brought in children. The foreign population peaked at 4.7 million in 1982. One third were Turks. This unplanned and unexpected settlement in a period of crisis became a major political issue, with none of the parties willing to face up to the inevitability of a multi-ethnic society. In the last few years, the migration balance has again been negative, as some migrants flee from unemployment and racism. The current level of 4.4 million foreign residents is likely to be maintained. Despite the well-organized system for temporary recruitment of guest-workers, the GFR has become a country of permanent settlement.

## The Migratory Process

This brief summary of temporary labor systems in six European countries can hardly do justice to the complexity of international labor migrations in the postwar period, but perhaps it suffices to show certain major features. First, it should be noted that virtually all the countries concerned have had migrants of varying types: guest-workers, colonial workers, skilled personnel moving between highly-developed countries and refugees. The latter do not move in search for work, but often find themselves doing the same kind of job as colonial workers or guest-workers. Secondly, all the countries dealt with above have tried guest-worker systems. In the case of Britain, Belgium and France, these systems were used early in the postwar period, and then abandoned in favor of spontaneous labor migration. Switzerland used a guest- worker system throughout the postwar economic expansion, while the Netherlands and the GFR introduced such systems in the late fifties and early sixties. Thirdly, all the countries examined stopped labor migration about the same time—following the "oil crisis" of 1973, when it became clear that a world recession was impending. The only exception is Britain, where labor migration had already been severely restricted through the Commonwealth Immigrants Act of 1962. The cause lay both in Britain's already stagnating economy and in the explosive racial tensions developing in the decaying inner cities. Fourthly, none of the countries expected or intended the guest- workers to become settlers. Employers and government of the recruiting countries had an interest in a flexible source of temporary labor. The states of the countries of origin of the workers accepted the system of temporary migration, because they saw it a palliative for unemployment, as well as a source of foreign exchange for their own economies through worker's remittances. The workers themselves generally hoped to save enough cash through three to five years work, to be able to buy land, livestock or machinery, or to set up a business. They were becoming temporary proletarians abroad to avoid permanent proletarianization in their own countries. So what went wrong? The answer lies in the dynamics of two simultaneous and interacting processes: the migratory process itself, and the process of restructuring of the world economy which is at present taking place.

The first phase of the migratory process was the phase of mass labor migration. The intention of temporary migration is common to the initial phase of most migratory movements—even to those seen in retrospect as permanent, such as movement to the USA, Latin America and Australia (See, Piore, 1979: Chapter 6, for the USA). Hence the correspondence of the migrants' aims with those of the employers and states of the receiving and sending countries. As time went on, many migrant workers found that it was impossible to earn and save enough to achieve their economic aims. Moreover, the deterioration of the political and economic situation in some of the countries of origin made an early return seem less and less feasible. As the prospect of going home receded, a life of nothing but hard work, frugality and social isolation seemed less acceptable. Workers started bringing in spouses and children, or starting new families. The second phase of the migratory process, the phase of family reunification, got under way. Family reunification usually did not imply a decision to settle permanently. Indeed it was sometimes seen as a way of speeding return, for family members often came as workers rather than just dependants. Family migration had its own logic: family housing and other needs raised migrants' cost of living, reducing savings yet further. Once children were born in Western Europe and started going to school, the prospect of return receded once again.

Family reunification contradicted the aims of the guest-worker system, and was initially rejected by the authorities of several countries. We have seen how competition for labor in the sixties, together with the employers' interest in a stable labor force, led to relaxation of regulations. The influences of multilateral agreements, within the OECD, the European Community, the Council of Europe and the Nordic Labor Market also played a part. The main cause of family reunification was simply migrants' refusal to accept the denial of the basic human right of living with their wives, husbands and children. Dependants were brought in legally where possible, illegally where the rights were refused. Once large-scale labor migration was established, family immigration became inevitable.

By the time labor migration was halted in the early seventies, the trend to family reunification was well established. The states of Western Europe hoped that stopping labor migration would cause large-scale return of both workers and dependants. Large numbers of workers did leave, but those who did stay brought in dependants, so that the total migrant population became stabilized or even grew. Once migrant families become established, and start to build communities, once their children are born and go to school in Western European cities, it is inevitable that most will stay. Since, on the other hand, the unplanned nature of this process, in a situation of crisis and racism, leads to marginalization of the migrant populations, the third phase of the migratory process is not only the phase of permanent settlement but also the phase of the development of new ethnic minorities. This is likely to have important and permanent consequences for West European societies.

### The Political Economy of the Guest-Worker System

What were the specific trends in the development of the world economy which made guest-worker systems an appropriate form of labor mobilization for Western Europe for 1945 to 1974, and then made them superfluous?* In a nutshell: the former period was one of concentration of capital and production, the latter period was one of global dispersal of industrial production, accompanied by revolutionary innovations in communications and control techniques. These new trends have transformed the role of the old industrial centers in the global division of labor, and have caused new labor migrations. The migrants of the previous phase, who are now settlers, have been left by the wayside.

The expansion from 1945 to the early seventies saw the most rapid and sustained development of production in history, with world capitalist output doubling in the period from 1952-68 alone (Glyn and Harrison, 1980:5). The causes of the long boom were complex and closely interdependent: the dominance of US capital, which emerged from the war, allowed a restructuring of financial and commodity markets. US corporations reorganized large sectors of industrial production in Western Europe, while its growing influence in newly independent Third World secured cheap raw materials and agricultural products. The advanced sectors of capital became transnational, as they strove to integrate production, trade and finance on a world scale. The weakening of the labor movement through fascism and war (especially in the later "economic miracle" countries of West Germany, Italy and Japan) kept wages relatively low in relation to productivity growth in the early postwar years, encouraging high rates of investment. Postwar reconstruction led to high demand for goods of all kind. Rearmament, the "Korea boom" and the cold war revived demand when it began to show signs of flagging, and this role was later taken over by the consumer boom of the sixties and by the opportunities for renewal of fixed capital due to the expansion of new highly-mechanized industries.

On average, employment in the advanced capitalist countries grew by about one percent per year during the period of expansion. This seems little compared to the rate of capital accumulation (the stock of the means of production grew by about 6% per year [Glyn and Harrison, 1980:5-7]). Yet growth of labor supply was an essential precondition for capital accumulation. If no new workers had been available, employers wanting to expand production would have had to offer higher wages to attract labor away from competitors. These, in turn, would have had to offer higher wages to retain labor. The resulting increased rate of inflation would have led to a stop-go economy, reducing economic growth and causing an early end to the boom (See, Kindleberger, 1967). An OECD study summed up the function of labor migration as follows:

> To permit the industrialized countries to fill job vacancies with reduced upward pressure on wages and profits. This added to national output in those countries and protected their competitive position in world trade. (OECD, 1978:7, 2/17)

Labor migration was not the only source of additional supply. It complemented the increased industrial employment of women, inter-

---

*This article deals with Western Europe, but the concentration of labor in the industrial metropoles in this period applied also to North America and Japan, as did the subsequent global restructuring of production.

nal rural-urban migration, absorption of returning soldiers or colonial officials, and of refugees and displaced persons. However, labor migration, particularly of the guest-worker type, was a particularly useful source of labor: it could be readily controlled by the state and employers, it was flexible and mobile. Above all, the migrants, as newcomers lacking rights and often without much education and training, could be steered towards the unskilled, dirty, hard jobs, that nobody else wanted to do. Migration prevented wages in these sectors rising as they would otherwise inevitably have done. Migrant labor was, on the whole, a special type of labor: it eased social mobility for some indigenous workers, and at the same time made possible the widespread deskilling of industrial work through Tayloristic methods of mass production (conveyor-line work, piece work, shift-work) which was so significant in the sixties (this argument is developed in Castles, Booth and Wallace, 1984: Chapter 5). This role of migrant labor became particularly important in the sixties, as indigenous labor forces began to decline through previous low birth-rates, increasing length of education and (in some countries) conscription of young men for military service.

There was, of course, a conceivable alternative: increased rationalization to replace labor with machinery. Some economists argued that import of labor was economically harmful, because it reduced the incentive for this. This argument forgets that the capital for rationalization has to come from past profits. A tight labor market which kept wages up and profits down would also hinder rationalization. In the boom period there was in fact a correlation between economic growth, increase of labor supply and improvement of productivity. In the GFR and Switzerland the labor force grew fast and there were also large investments in modern plants with high productivity. In the long run, the economy grew steadily and fast, and wages increased too. In Britain, on the other hand, the labor force grew little, the profit rate remained too low to induce investment in new and more productive plants, economic growth was slow and sporadic, and wages in the long run increased less than in the GFR and Switzerland. the effect of abundant labor supply in the long run was not to keep wages down absolutely, but to keep down their relative share in the national income, allowing profits and investments to remain high.

So why the sudden turn-around in the mid seventies? The most obvious cause was the "oil crisis" and the subsequent recession, which led to unemployment and persistent economic, social and, often, political crisis in the countries of Western Europe. Underlying this were two more significant factors. The first has already been dealt with: as the migratory process matured, the economic benefits of employing migrants became eroded. Family reunification reduced the flexibility and mobility of migrant labor, and created a demand for social capital investment in housing, education, health and social amenities. Where this need was not met—and that was the rule—urban decay, social tension and political conflict were the result. The states of Western Europe were becoming concerned with the strains of the shift from

71

labor migration to settlement, which were seen as the responsibility of the state, rather than of the employers. These were becoming increasingly difficult to manage, in view of inflation and fiscal crisis. The emphasis of state discourse was shifting from labor market policy to issues of public order. The question raised by labor market authorities, employers' associations and international organization like the ILO and the OECD, was increasingly: "is it not more rational to move the machines to the workers, rather than the workers to the machines?" And this was just what was beginning to happen anyway.

Herein lies the second factor: in the postwar boom, the dynamism of Western European capitalism had led to high rates of capital accumulation, caused in part by the inflow of US investments, especially in West Germany. The result, by the end of the sixties, was an over-accumulation of capital, leading to a high demand for other factors of production. There were simply too many factories requiring labor, raw materials, transport, ancilliary services, land, water and air, in a small geographical area. This meant that the costs of all these production factors was soaring (compare Grahl, 1983). A further consequence of over-industrialization was pollution and destruction of the environment, leading to emission controls, which further increased costs.

Similar strains were emerging in the USA and Japan. In the current phase of restructuring which stems from these problems, the direction and character of capital flows has changed. US and transnational capital are now being invested more in areas of the Third World—the so-called newly industrializing countries (or NICS)—and in less industrialized parts of Europe and the US, rather than in the traditional industrial centers. The recycling of petrodollars in the period of high oil prices following 1973 played a major part in this restructuring. Western European countries, which were major labor importers in the postwar expansion period, have now become major capital exporters. With transnational enterprises (themselves often a product of previous US investment, or of fusion between US and other national capital) a new division of labor is permitting the transfer of labor- intensive production processes to other countries, in the low-wage offshore production areas of the Third World. The industrial production processes remaining in the core areas of the world economy (Western Europe, North America, Japan) are characterized by increased automation and intensification of work.

At the same time, a further important trend affects the structure of the labor markets in these areas: the development of what has been called "global control capability" in the major cities of the capitalist world (Sassen-Koob, 1985). This refers to the concentration of functions of management, communication, research and development, as well as finance, in cities like London, New York, Frankfurt, Paris, Tokyo, Sydney and Singapore. The result is a job-market of highly-trained and well-paid specialists, but also of a myriad of diverse service workers, to provide for their sophisticated consumer needs. Such services have to be provided where they are consumed, and cannot therefore be developed to low-wage countries. Moreover, there is a current trend towards re-establishment of certain forms of labor-intensive production in the metropoles. Growing unemployment and marginalization of certain categories of labor (especially women, youth and ethnic minorities) provides a basis for the growth of work-forms peripheral to and dependant on large companies: for example computer outwork, garment manufacture in sweatshops or at home (mainly by ethnic minority women), widespread employment of youths as casual labor in shops and catering. A new segmentation of the labor market is developing, which can be examined both at the global and local levels (See, Sassen-Koob, 1985; Phizacklea, 1985; Mitter, 1986).

## Perspectives

In conclusion, we shall address ourselves to two questions: first what are the consequences of the developments described in this article for the former guest-workers? Secondly, what developments are to be observed in the international labor migrations, and what perspectives are there for the continued utilization of the guest-worker systems?

The guest-workers systems of Western Europe are dead, except for the use of seasonal workers in France and Switzerland. The guest-workers are no longer with us; either they have gone or they have been transmogrified into settlers and marginalized into ethnic minorities. After two or three decades of migration, foreign workers had become an integral part of the labor force. The segmentation of the labor market—itself a product of the discriminatory guest-worker system—made it impossible to dispense with them quickly when the downturn came. Most could not easily be replaced by indigenous workers, even when unemployment reached record levels at the beginning of the eighties. Employers have, therefore, usually not been in favor of policies of mass repatriation, fearing that it would lead to acute labor shortages in certain areas, and hence to upward pressure on wages.

States have developed two main strategies to manage the ethnic minorities in the crisis. First, workers belonging to ethnic minorities are being used as a buffer to cushion partially other workers from the economic effects of the crisis. This is particularly easy in countries where migrants still lack sociopolitical rights. National preferences in hiring, and refusal or withdrawal of work permits ensure that foreign workers are the first to go. Moreover, the structure of the labor process ensures higher unemployment for minority workers. They are generally employed in the occupations and sectors hardest hit by the process of restructuring. Members of ethnic minorities in Western Europe are extremely vulnerable to dismissal during recession, and generally have high rates of unemployment (See, Castles, Booth and Wallace, 1984:143-9).

Secondly, the New Right in Western Europe is developing an ideological and political offensive against the minorities. In some cases (notably Britain, Frances and the GFR) this has had a significant impact on state policy. As working-class living standards decline, as the inner cities decay, as the destruction of the environment becomes ever more evident, as the threat of war looms larger in people's minds, as youth shows less and less interest in established political institutions, the state is confronted with a crisis of legitimacy. State efforts to reassert control are leading to a concentration of power in the executive, an erosion of democratic institutions, a decline in the role of political parties and a curtailment of civil liberties. One method of gaining public support for such strategies is the construction and projection of alleged threats to society presented by the ethnic minorities. A recent British study refers to a "racialization of state policies in all areas of social life" (CCCS, 1982). the construction of the "foreigner problem" in the GFR is another example (Castles, 1985). Media and politicians present an image of ethnic minorities who take away other workers' jobs, sponge off social security, cause the housing problem, overwhelm the schools, and generally swamp "our" society and culture. Minority youth threaten public order through muggings, drugs and attacks on the police. Alien extremists create social unrest through violent demonstrations and terrorism. The Islamic minorities in France, Germany and Britain are portrayed as a threat to occidental Christian civilization.

The wind has been sown by the parliamentary right, whose assertions of national interests are generally not openly racist. The corn is being reaped by the extreme right and neo-fascists like Le Pen in France, the National Front in Britain, the NPD and terroristic gangs linked with it in the GFR. This revival of extremist violence may yet prove the most significant long- term impact of temporary migrant labor systems on Western European societies.

But the cause is not the employment of migrants in itself, but rather, the attempt to treat migrants purely as economic men and women, and to separate labor power and other human attributes. Because permanent immigration was not expected, and the states concerned refused to take the necessary steps to provide the housing and social amenities needed for orderly settlement, migration has exacerbated some of the underlying problems of Western European societies. It is easier now to blame the victims than to come to grips with the causes.

This brings us to our second question. The current restructuring of the world economy is giving rise to new migrations. Three main trends may be identified: first the movement of workers to new industrial areas in Third World countries, e.g., to the offshore production areas of Southeast Asia and Latin America. This is mainly internal rural-urban migration of a spontaneous kind, and the majority of migrant workers are women. The second is the migration of workers from Third World countries to oil countries carrying out industrialization programs, e.g., from Pakistan to Saudi Arabia, from Turkey to Libya. This is generally within rigid guest-worker programs, prohibiting settlement and family reunification. In some cases, transnational corporations act as intermediaries.* Many of these contract wor-

---

*The West German construction giant, Philip Holzmann, A.G. has contracted with the

kers have been sent home, following the recent decline in the fortunes of OPEC. Will this type of guest-worker employment shift towards settlement in time? I argue that that is likely in the long run although the governments concerned seem determined to prevent it, and are not likely to be swayed by niceties concerning human rights. The third current trend is the migration of labor to the "world cities" where the concentration of "global control capability" leads to demand both for highly-qualified workers and for low-skilled industrial and service workers (See, Sassen-Koob, 1985). This last form is at present, for the most part, not taking place within guest-worker systems.

---

Chinese Government to employ Chinese workers on building sites in NICs and OPEC countries. The workers are on fixed-term contracts, and their wages are paid to the Chinese Government, which passes them on (in part) to the workers in China.

# REFERENCES

Castles, S. 1985 "The Guests Who Stayed—The Debate on 'Foreigners Policy' in the German Federal Republic", *International Migration Review*, 19(3), 517- 534.

Castles, S. with H. Booth and T. Wallace 1984 *Here for Good—Western Europe's New Ethnic Minorities*, London: Pluto Press.

Castles, S. and G. Kosack 1973-1985 *Immigrant Workers and Class Structure in Western Europe*, London: Oxford University Press.

Center for Contemporary Cultural Studies 1982 *The Empire Strikes Back—Race and Racism in 70s Britain*. London: Hutchinson.

Forchungserbund 1979 "Probleme der Ausländerbeschaftigung", *Intergierter Endbericht.*

Glyn, A. and J. Harrison 1980 *The British Economic Disaster.* London: Pluto Press.

Grahl, J. 1983 "Restructuring in West European Industry", *Capital and Class,* (19).

Hepple, B. 1968 *Race, Jobs and the Law in Britain,* London: Penguin.

Kindleberger, C.P. 1967 *Europe's Postwar Growth: The Role of Labour Supply,* Cambridge, Mass.: Harvard University Press.

Mitter, S. 1986 "Industrial Restructuring and Manufacturing Homework: Immigrant Women in the UK Clothing Industry", *Capital and Class,* (27).

Netherlands Scientific Council for Government Policy 1979 *Ethnic Minorities,* The Hague.

OECD 1978 *Migration Growth and Development,* Paris: OECD.

Office National d'Immigration 1968 *Statistiques d'Immigration,* Paris.

Phizacklea, A. 1985 "Minority Women and Restructuring: the Case of Britain, France and the Federal Republic of Germany". Paper presented at the conference on *Racial Minorities, Economic Restructuring and Urban Decline,* Center for Research in Ethnic Relations, University of Warwick.

Piore, M.J. 1979 *Birds of Passage—Migrant Labor and Industrial Societies,* Cambridge

SOPEMI 1984 SOPEMI—*Continuous Reporting System on Migration,* Paris: OECD.

SOPEMI—Netherlands 1985 *SOPEMI—Netherlands: Migration, Minorities and Policy in the Netherlands,* Amsterdam: Department of Human Geography, University of Amsterdam.

Sassen-Koob, A. 1985 "Capital Mobility and Labour Migration: Their Expression in Core Cities". Paper presented at the conference of *Racial Minorities, Economic Restructuring and Urban Decline.* Center for Research in Ethnic Relations, University of Warwick.

# A New Agenda in Multiculturalism

## 1. Signs of the Times

In the 70s and early 80s, there appeared to be a considerable measure of consensus in Australia on policies towards immigrants: they were to be permitted a large measure of cultural autonomy, while at the same time special institutions and measures were introduced to ensure access and equity and participation for all Australians irrespective of their origins. These policies—referred to collectively as multiculturalism—were endorsed and implemented (albeit in varying forms) by the major political parties, and appeared to enjoy broad public support. However, recent events indicate that this multicultural consensus is no longer uncontested, and that important changes are taking place, or are imminent:

— The first was the "Blainey Debate" of 1984, which questioned the nonracist immigration policy. Blainey's attack on Asian entries was supported by Bruce Ruxton of the Victorian RSL (Returned Servicemens' League), who has continued with an onslaught on Black South African immigration. This debate rapidly widened into an attack on multiculturalism, with considerable media airing through David Barnett's notorious article in *The Bulletin* (18 February 1986), and Des Keegan's scurrilous "National Affairs Column" in *The Australian*.

— An enormous amount of recent academic research in the disciplines of sociology, economics and education has gone into demonstrating that there is no such thing as migrant disadvantage, and that there is consequently no need for special policies in this area.[1] Most recently, the claim has been raised that it is now the Anglo working class who are becoming the "new self-deprived".[2]

— The Budget for 1986-87 announced considerable cuts in the multicultural area, notably the abolition of the Australian Institute of Multicultural Affairs (AIMA), the merger of the SBS with the ABC,* cuts in Commonwealth funding for English as a second language teaching and for the Multicultural Education Program, the closure or reduction in size of regional offices of the Department of Immigration and Ethnic Affairs (DIEA). The savings brought about by these measures was minor, so that it appeared that their real purpose was to ring in a change of policy.

---

*The Special Broadcasting Service (SBS) is a multicultural T.V. and radio network which broadcasts in the language of the ethnic communities. The Australian Broadcasting Commission (ABC) is the main public network.

---

This paper originally appeared as *Multicultural Australia Papers*. Richmond Vic, Australia: Clearing House on Migration Issues, 1987. number 61

Archbishop Penman (Chairman of AIMA) spoke of the abandonment of multiculturalism in key areas, while ethnic groups protested vocally.[3]

— In the first half of 1986, a major review of multicultural services and programs was carried out on behalf of the DIEA. By the time its findings were published the ground had been cut away from beneath it by the Budget measures. The ROMAMPAS or Jupp Report[4] became an embarrassment, to be thrown in the memory hole of history. At the same time, other reviews were being carried out: of the Victorian Ethnic Affairs Commission[5] and of the Multicultural and Ethnic Affairs Commission of Western Australia.

— The disenchantment of the ethnic communities with ALP policies became ever-more evident. The marginal premier of NSW, Barry Unsworth, emphasised the significance of the ethnic vote, and called for more sensitivity in Canberra. One result was the dismissal in February of the unpopular Minister of Immigration and Ethnic Affairs, Hurford, and his replacement by Mick Young. The fact that Mick Young is also ALP Party Chairman shows how seriously ALP strategists are taking the ethnic vote in this pre-election period.

— The only substantive innovations have been the establishment of an Office of Multicultural Affairs (OMA) in the Prime Minister's Department and the appointment of an Advisory Council on Multicultural Affairs to advise the Prime Minister.[6] OMA's exact function has yet to be clarified, but will include vetting Federal Government Departments' Access and Equity Statements. But the main function of OMA and the Advisory Council is no doubt to convince ethnic communities that the Government is still committed to multiculturalism.

## 2. The Roots of Multiculturalism

Do these events add up to a major shift in ethnic affairs policies in Australia? Do they herald a move away from multiculturalism? And if so, will the course be back towards assimilationism, or in a completely new direction? I will argue here that an important change is taking place, but that despite the growing vocalisation of racism and the call for regressive moves, the direction is not simply backwards. Rather new models for ethnic affairs are emerging in response to:

— the maturing of the migratory process (particularly for postwar European immigrants);
— changes in economic, social and political conditions in Australia;
— changes in the character of current immigration.

To understand these changes, it is necesssary to take an historical view of postwar immigration and the development of multicultural policies.

The aims of the postwar immigration program were to increase the population, for strategic reasons, and to increase the labor force and the domestic market for economic reasons. The creation of a polyethnic society was never in anybody's mind. The plan was to bring in British migrants, or, failing this, others of "assimilable types". A large proportion of the migrant workers who helped build Australia's infrastructure and manufacturing base in the fifties and sixties were Southern Europeans. By the sixties, it was evident that assimilation was not taking place: persistent ethnic segregation in the workplace and to some extent in housing, the maintenance of ethnic languages and cultures, the development of ethnic welfare and educational initiatives, the growth of ethnic media, were all factors indicating the unplanned emergence of a pluralist society. Teachers, welfare workers and academics pointed out to the government that migrants were not assimilating, that they could and should not be expected to do so and that the continuation of an assimlationist policy was leading to a crisis, particularly in the welfare and education system. The call was raised for recognition of a situation of "cultural pluralism".[7]

From the outset, there were two ways of looking at this: one was to define pluralism in terms of ethnic identity. Migrants constituted themselves as groups and sought to maintain their languages and culture, in order to gain material support and psychological protection in a new environment. Clinging to "primordial attachments" was a defense mechanism for groups whose experience of modernisation had taken the dramatic form of migration. The acceptance of cultural difference and the recognition of the ethnic group and its leadership (however defined) were the consequence of this approach, which is embodied in the academic work of Jerzy Zubrzycki and the policy approach of the Galbally Report of 1978.

The other way of looking at the situation was to emphasise the way the power and class structures of Australian society marginalised certain groups of migrant workers, and turned them into ethnic minorities. Work and residential segregation was both a result of their economic role, and a guarantee of its continuation. Neither the motivations of the migrants nor the interests of their employers were conducive to assimilation. Cultural maintenance and development of community structures were reactions to processes of structural exclusion, connected with the role of migrant labor in the Australian economy. The cultivation of ethnic languages, traditions and customs was seen as a mere surface expression of deeper-going conflicts. The emphasis on ethnic disadvantage and the special problems of particular migrant workers groups was expressed through the work of Jean Martin in the '70s, as well as through policy documents such as the NSW Ethnic Affairs Commission report *Participation* (1978) or the Victorian EAC's manifesto *Access and Equity* (1983).

This dualism in the understanding of the emerging ethnic pluralism corresponds with a dualism in the concept of multiculturalism that started to emerge after Al Grassby's lecture about the "multicultural society of the future" and "the family of the nation" in 1973. This dualism perhaps explains how it was possible that the slogan of multiculturalism could be maintained by such diverse governments as those of Whitlam, Fraser and Hawke. The dualism has at its one pole the concept of multiculturalism as a view of society, as an ideology that postulates a manner in which society is or should be organised. The other pole is the concept of multiculturalism as a principle to guide social policy.

Multiculturalism as an *ideology of society* calls for an acceptance of cultural pluralism and of the legitimacy of an ongoing ethnic diversity within Australian society. There is an expectation that cultural particularity will be maintained over the generations for an indefinite period. One central problem of this culturalist approach—seen clearly by proponents such as Zubrzycki—is the tension between ethnic pluralism and the cohesiveness of society as a whole. How can a nation be defined, if not in terms of ethnic identity? How are core values and acceptable behavoral forms to be worked out if the hegemony of Anglo-Australian culture is no longer accepted? The problems of poly-ethnic states are neither new nor unique in the world, but they are a new departure in the history of Australia as an outpost of the British Empire. As an ideology, multiculturalism requires radical changes in thinking and behavior, and for all its apparent acceptance, has so far merely scratched the surface of Australia's institutional structures.[8]

The second problem of the culturalist approach concerns the tension between the legitimacy of cultural maintenance and the role of culture in regulating access to economic resources and political power. Proficiency in language, use of elaborated codes, manipulation of cultural symbols determine entry to upper-level occupational positions, both directly and indirectly (through their role in allowing people to gain educational credentials). The role of culture with regard to the transference of class position from one generation to the next has been a major theme of sociology for many years. Clearly, the problem is even more acute when ethnic and class cultures interact. The state can legislate for access and equity in its own services and can enact antidiscrimination legislation, but it cannot, in the current political framework, prevent cultural markers being used in the non-state sector. This is still the main area where class position is determined. So policies of accepting cultural pluralism may actually be detrimental to the equal opportunity of migrants' children: they become locked into what are seen as "sub-cultures" by those with power, and this blocks social mobility. Proponents of culturalism are aware of this problem, but examine it in terms of "cultural deprivation", i.e. the deficiencies of the individual, rather than the structural barriers of society.[9]

Multiculturalism as a *principle of social policy* was based on social research on the situation of migrants, which concentrated on their actual situation in Australian society. This approach did not look at migrants in general terms of ethnicity and culture, but rather tried to identify particular areas of socio-economic disadvantage. The work of Jean Martin on the economic and social condition of migrants played a large part in the development of this approach.[10] The basic problems experienced by migrants were seen not as a result of cultural dissonance, but as a consequence of the segmentation of the Australian labor market, and the location of Southern European migrant workers in the manual working class.[11] In recent years, a lot of work has gone into the development of this approach and into linking the three dimensions of inequality: ethnicity, class and gender.[12]

In this context, the task of multiculturalism is that of identifying and attacking those structural factors in Australian society which stigmatise and disadvantage migrant workers and migrant women. Social policies must be designed to change institutions, in order to make them fit the needs of all Australians (i.e. including the one fifth of the population who are of non-English speaking background). The issue becomes one of equal opportunities in a non-egalitarian society, and the emphasis is on the problems of migrants in obtaining full and equal participation in the political, social and economic system, rather than on identity and distinctiveness.[13] This approach involves defining particular migrant groups as ethnic minorities, and demanding rights and social justice for them. The Ethnic Affairs Commissions which have been set up in four states since 1978 are at the forefront in attempting to implement policies to achieve equal opportunity at work, in health and education, and in the provision of government services. The policy of "mainstreaming" advocated particularly in NSW and South Australia is a clear consequence of this way of tackling the problem: all political and social institutions should be appropriate to a multicultural society, as opposed to the Galbally approach which tended to encourage specialised (and often marginalised) institutions for ethnic groups. Of course, here too my earlier remark applies: the capacity of the state for changing the well-worn ethnocentric structures of the private sector is limited. Indeed, even within the state apparatus, the resistance to change is daunting.

Now I do not want to suggest that there is a clear polarity between culturalists and proponents of social justice. As Laki Jayasuriya has pointed out: "All reports dealing with migrants' settlement and ethnic affairs have straddled the twin issues of equality and identity—espoused the need to provide for equality of opportunity as a matter of right belonging to all citizens as well as the 'right' to cultural maintenance."[14] The difference is rather one of emphasis: Zubrzycki, Galbally and AIMA (at least until 1984) stressed identity, while Jean Martin, the "Wollongong School" and the Ethnic Affairs Commissions stressed equality. Moreover, there is an alternative way of looking at multiculturalism as social policy: i.e. to see it as a mechanism of social control, in which the state constructs ethnic petit-bourgeoisies as a cheap way of controlling migrant labor and youth.[15] I have no time for a discussion of the detailed issues involved here. What I have said so far should be enough to indicate the complexities and ambiguities of multiculturalism. There may have been a political consensus that it was a good thing, but there was never a consensus about what it actually was.

### 3. The New Conditions

Multiculturalism was not just a natural evolution out of the failed policy of assimilationism. It was a response to a set of particular conditions which were apparent in the 70s:
- the postwar migratory process had made Australia into a polyethnic society. The Southern European migrants were forming communities culturally, economically and socially distinct from the rest of the population; the coming of age of second and third generations was not leading to the disappearance of ethnic identity;[16]
- growing involvement of migrants in economic, political and cultural life, was leading to increased self-confidence and demands for ethnic rights and participation;
- the Australian economy had been through a long phase of expansion, and a large proportion of the population had experienced real improvements in income and social security. It was generally accepted that the postwar immigration program had contributed substantially to this expansion, and had therefore benefited all major social groups;
- there appeared to be a decline in xenophobia and racism among the Australian population. This was based in part on acceptance of ethnic lifestyles through contact in the cities, partly on a new perspective on ideas of Anglo superiority, as Britain declined. The realisation that Australia must come to terms with its position close to Asia, and growing admiration for Asian economic success also contributed. This trend was often superficial and did not affect all Australians.

Do these conditions still hold good in the mid-80s? It is necessary to examine certain changes, if we are to understand the context of current debates on the future of multiculturalism.

### 3.1 Changes in the migratory process

The Southern European migrant workers, whose concerns were central in the development of multiculturalism, have aged. Most of them came in the '50s and '60s, and have reached or are nearing the end of their working lives. The result is a new discussion on the problems of the ethnic aged.[17] As second and third generations grow up, complete their education and enter the labor market, there is a shift in problems and perceptions of them.[18] Galbally-type multiculturalism, with its emphasis on ethnic group and state support of self-help, appears as a "first-generation strategy",[19] which is increasingly irrelevant to the current situation. The central issues are equality of opportunity for all and social justice for groups which have been marginalised.

The forms of political mobilisation of ethnic minorities are shifting. The young people who have come through the Australian educational system do not express their interests through ethnic organisations to the same extent as their parents. Many of them are "inside the system": welfare and educational professionals with networks linking both ethnic and mainstream institutions. This has led to a questioning of the concept of the "ethnic vote" as a political factor.

The process of differentiation of ethnic groups continues: On the one hand, differences in employment and residential patterns between different origin groups persists. On the other, social differentiation within each group is becoming more obvious, so that average or aggregate data are increasingly meaningless.[20] As first generation migrants leave the labor process, there are changes in the occupational and residential patterns of ethnic groups. Are the new migrant groups (particularly Asians) replacing Southern Europeans in a process of ethnic succession? Are we looking at a process of upward social mobility of migrants, or a process of inter-generational mobility, or is the apparent change simply a response to economic restructuring? Probably all these factors are interrelated in a complex way.

## 3.2 Changes in the.economic situation

Australian manufacturing shed a quarter of a million jobs from 1973 to 1983. During the same period a net total of 449,700 new jobs was created in the economy as a whole, the big growth sector being Community Services (381,200 newjobs).[21] The main decline has been in the sectors where European migrant workers were concentrated, while the growth has been in areas where lack of language proficiency and educational credentials makes access difficult for them. Many migrant workers have been marginalised out of the workforce, either through lack of job prospects, or through industrial illnesses and injuries. Economic restructuring is a complex process, involving not only shifts in employment patterns and skill requirements, but also changes in organisational forms of the labor process, such as the growth of subcontracting, self-employment and the black economy. Disadvantaged groups such as unskilled workers, women workers and youth are likely to be hardest hit, the result being high rates of unemployment, or development of particularly exploitative forms of work. The changing economic context affects migrants in three dimensions:
— changes in the material situation of existing migrant workers;
— changes in public attitudes towards migration;
— changes in the type of migration encouraged by Government and employers.

## 3.3 Changes in migration policies

In the early '80s, immigration policy was shifting towards an emphasis on family reunion and refugee programs, rather than on labor migration. At the same time, as Australian wages have fallen relative to traditional labor supplying countries in Europe, it has become evident that any substantial increase in immigrant numbers must come from Asia. Over the last few years the ruling class appears to have been in the process of redefining its attitudes towards immigration. The CEDA report[22] and the response to it among business people and politicians indicates a return to the idea of mass labor immigration as a way of securing economic growth. Kerry Packer has called for 200,000 new migrants per year, while Brian Burke, the Premier of Western Australia wants Asian migrants to develop the arid North. Yet this call for more migrants has been linked to an attack on multiculturalism: the Asians are regarded as desirable migrants because they work hard, have the "right attitudes" and appear capable of assimilation (defined as adaptation to the needs of free market industrialism rather than in cultural terms). So, paradoxically, New Right opponents of multiculturalism like Lauchlan Chipman can call for more Asian immigrants.[23] However, it is not Indo-Chinese refugees who are wanted, but well-educated people from India, Singapore or Hong Kong, who, moreover, often bring capital with them. The corollary is a move away from an immigration policy emphasising family reunification and humanitarian considerations.

The shift in economic conditions has changed the way that popular attitudes towards migration and migrants are expressed. Once again, migrant workers are seen as competitors for scarce jobs and a potential threat to wages and conditions. This feeling is all the more prevalent in the working class, who have most reason to fear competition. A recent statement on immigration policy by the Australian Council of Trade Unions calls for continued emphasis on entries of refugees and family members of persons resident in Australia, while rejecting migration as a means of solving general or long-term shortages of labor. The ACTU is therefore against increases in the skilled labor migrant category.[24]

As so often in Australian history, working-class fears of a threat to conditions can easily become articulated in the form of racism (in this case directed particularly against Asians). The malaise at Australia's political and economic decline is taking on the form of the "common sense" demand for defending the interests and the traditional values of the Anglo working class. The racist backlash led by Bruce Ruxton is indicative of this trend.

## 4. Towards a New Agenda

There is no doubt, that the conditions for multicultural policies have changed substantially in the last three or four years. The reviews, the Budget cuts and the change in Minister mentioned above are responses to these shifts, but they appear tentative, and lacking in clear direction. The budget cuts marked the end of the culturalist agenda which had been set by the Galbally Report and the Fraser government, but they simultaneously removed the basis of many of the recommendations of the ROMAMPAS Report, before these were even published. ROMAMPAS was expected by the DIEA to shape the new agenda for multiculturalism within the idiom of Social-democratic social policy, but it was still- born. So where does that leave us?

It seems to me that the culturalist position in the multicultural debate of the '70s and early '80s is losing its relevance as a guide to policy. Culturalism of the Zubrzycki-Galbally type is on the way out: first because its basis as a "first-generation strategy" has been superseded; secondly because its message is no longer contested at the superficial level of rhetoric on diversity and equal rights. At present there would appear to be two options: a "new laissez-faire" in ethnic affairs, or a reassertion of the policy of social justice for minority groups. In each, social science plays an important part in helping to define issues and indicate policies. Of course, the choice of which type of social science is to be funded still lies with those with political and economic power, so it is not a question of the best paradigm influencing policy. Rather shifts in political, economic and social forces determine the predominance of social science paradigms.

## 4.1 The New Laissez-Faire

The paradigm which appears to be gaining ground as a new "conventional wisdom" (in Galbraith's sense) is one whose answer to the question about the specific problems of ethnic minorities in Australian society, is that there are no ethnic minorities and no specific problems. This position is closely linked to the neo-classical human capital approach in economics. Its proponents have been based mainly with the Bureau of Labour Market Studies and the Centre for Economic Policy Research at the ANU.[25] The CEDA study, referred to above is similar in its conceptual framework, although concerned more directly with immigration policy. A closely related approach in sociology, based on quantitative work with Census or large-scale survey data, is best known through the work of ANU researchers such as Broom, Jones, McAllister, Kelly and Evans.[26] The conclusions arrived at, using highly aggregated data combined with methods of regression analysis which homogenise diverse migrant experiences, are that migrants have no major disadvantages concerning work, income and social position. The paradigm claims that migrants merely have short-term adaptation problems in Australian society, which they rapidly overcome. A very high degree of inter-generational mobility is discovered. An extension of this work in the educational field finds that the children of migrants are doing very well, and that it is the children of working-class Australians who are now deprived. However, they are "self-deprived": working class Australians lack the right attitudes towards work, risk-taking and education, and their family discipline is too weak. By comparison, most migrants (particularly Asians) are successful because of their "ethnic motivation" and strong family discipline.[27] Those who are not successful, are victims of individual disabilities or inadequacies.

To put it in simple terms, this paradigm asserts that "at the aggregate level. . .migrants in the Australian labor market do as well as persons born in Australia after an initial period of adjustment."[28] They do well because they are willing (or constrained by their situation as newcomers) to make "human capital investments". Australian workers, by contrast, are bludgers who expect a hand-out from the state, and whose trade-union attitudes are a facade for unwillingness to work. Students from working-class Australian homes are victims of their own "ocker attitudes" which make them disruptive and lazy. The policy consequences of this approach are obvious: the state should do as little as possible, and leave everything to the market. Social policy is harmful because it hinders the functioning of free market mechanisms.

The Federal Government and the DIEA appear to have bought this approach.[29] One consequence is an expansionist labor migration policy. Another is a reduction in multicultural programs which actually intervene to change institutional structures, or to set up special services for migrants and ethnic minorities. The Budget cuts were typical for this trend. Of course, current financial constraints provide a convincing rationale for such cuts, but they are not the main reason. At the same time, a useful ideology has been found to justify the policy change. It is summed up in the word "mainstreaming"—originally coined by the NSW Ethnic Affairs Commission to indicate the need for structural change in all areas of Government. Now the Federal Government uses "mainstreaming" as a cover for a new policy of noninterventionism. The official rationale for cutting ESL teaching and the Multicultural Education Program was that special measures were no longer necessary, as the mainstream systems were now capable of doing the job.[30] On this basis, multicultural services and programs can gradually be cut away by the simple official finding that they are no longer necessary. Migrant parents and the teachers of their children did not share this view.

At the same time, political considerations—the "ethnic vote", which no-one quite knows whether to believe in or not—make the maintaining of the rhetoric of multiculturalism essential. Hence the establishment of an Office of Multicultural Affairs in the Prime Minister's Department as the keeper of this Holy Grail in March 1986. It remains to be seen whether the functionaries of OMA will be satisfied with this role.

What this approach seems to boil down to is not a return to assimilationism, but rather a new sort of laissez-faire in ethnic affairs: cultural diversity of the "spaghetti and polka" type is seen as inevitable and acceptable and no longer a policy problem. The economic and social integration of migrants is to be left to market mechanisms, in the framework of an affirmative multicultural ideology, which has no major consequences in terms of costs or institutional change. All this fits well with a new policy of increased labor migration: by denying the need for special programs, the laissez-faire approach helps keep additional labor cheap.

## 4.2 Social Justice for Minority Groups

A social justice approach to the situation of migrant workers in Australia is not new—it is a continuation of the tradition of social democratic policy which started in the Whitlam era and has been maintained in the work of the Ethnic Affairs Commissions. But there is clearly a need for a redefinition of the problems and a search for solutions, in the light of the changing context which I described above. There is a new task for the social sciences: in the '70s it was valuable to look at "migrant disadvantage" or "the economic conditions of migrants". In the late '80s, such a task can only have an ideological function, due to the process of differentiation between and within migrant groups. The result today is meaningless average data, which mask problems rather than reveal them.

The role of social research today is to find out which groups have become marginalised, in the context of the interrelating processes of the maturing of migration and economic restructuring. Clearly in doing this we are relating the dimensions of ethnicity, gender and class, and we find that many migrants are not in marginalised positions, and many non-migrants are. It is essential to identify ethnic and other minorities, and to understand the mechanisms which lead to marginalisation. The methodology of this type of social research is different to that of the approach outlined above. General statistics may help to describe problems, but they do nothing to explain them. There is a need for a qualitative and longitudinal approach, which relates the global dimensions of inequality to the specific life experience of members of disadvantaged groups. Such work has been carried out, most notably by the Research and Policy Division of the Victorian Ethnic Affairs Commission, by some University research institutes and—just before its demise—by AIMA. We are not starting with a tabula rasa; it is clear enough which groups are most at risk:—the Southern European labor migrants of the fifties and sixties,who got locked into manual manufacturing jobs, and have been hard-hit by restructuring;
— the Middle East migrants and Indo-Chinese refugees of the seventies and eighties, who had trouble entering a labor market hit by recession;
— aged migrants, who are often affected by economic hardship and social isolation upon leaving the labor force;
— migrant youth, particularly affected by youth unemployment;
— people of non-European origin (sometimes called the 'visible minorities'), who are the victims of racial stigmatisation and discrimination. This is a situation shared by recent non-European migrants and Australia's Aboriginal population.
On the basis of such work it is possible to suggest policy changes, aimed at combatting structural factors which cause disadvantage, dealing with specific forms of social hardship and economic deprivation, as well as upgrading the education and skills of disadvantaged groups. The targeting of policies on specific minority groups is particularly important in an economic situation which precludes blanket approaches

to social policy. It is clear that this approach requires a substantial increase in state intervention and affirmative action, to improve the situation of minorities. This is likely to meet with little support from employers, or from Government treasurers concerned about the cost aspects. It is a policy that cannot be justified on the neo-classical economic postulates, which are so fashionable, even within the ALP.

The precondition for such work, however is a clear definition of the aims to be achieved. The rhetoric of multiculturalism from Galbally to ROMAMPAS is full of principles calling for "access and equity", "equitable participation" and the like. Upon close examination, most of these statements are limited to the call for equal opportunity for all, irrespective of people's specific needs and starting chances. There is little discussion of the issue of equality of outcomes—not surprising in a society whose central principle is inequality in ownership and income. Jayasuriya recommends the adoption of Rawls' radical liberal approach to social justice which calls for equality in civil liberties; equality of opportunity for advancement; and positive discrimination in favor of the underprivileged to ensure equity, i.e. fair shares for all.[31] Jayasuriya therefore calls for

"a new model of multiculturalism: a minority group rights model attuned to tne needs of the emerging future—the needs of the second and third generation ethnic minorities, the non-Caucasian groups, the increasingly articulate and militant women, and the ethnic aged....Multiculturalism must be seen as a vehicle of change powered by the ideals of social justice".

At the political level, a similar demand is raised in the "social justice strategy" of the Victorian ALP Government. The recent review of the Victorian Ethnic Affairs Commission re-affirmed the policies of the Commission in the light of this political program.[32] The call for social justice for ethnic minorities may seem to run counter to the tide of pragmatism in the crisis- ridden Australia of the late '80s, but it seems the only way forward, if a genuine policy of multiculturalism is to be maintained.

Perhaps the next step could be the declaration of a National Minorities Policy, as was done by the Netherlands Government in the early '80s. This was based on a Report by the Netherlands Scientific Council for Government Policy, which identified minority groups (including migrants from former colonies, Southern European migrant workers, gypsies and caravan dwellers) and proposed legal frameworks and policies for the achievement of their rights.[33] Obviously, the problems and the solutions for Australia cannot be the same as for the Netherlands, but the declaration of a minorities program, with a commitment to fundamental change, is a precedent which could and should be followed.

## Notes

1. For a summary of some of this work and a discussion of its methodology see: A. Jakubowicz and S. Castles, "The Inherent Subjectivity of the Apparently Objective in Research on Ethnicity and Class," in: *Journal of Intercultural Studies*, 1/87.
2. B. Bullivant, *Are Anglo-Australian Students becoming the New Self-Deprived in*

*Comparison with Ethnics?* Melbourne, Monash University, 1986.

3. See S. Castles, M. Kalantzis and B. Cope, "W(h)ither multiculturalism?" in: *Australian Society,* October 1986.

4. DIEA, *Don't Settle for Less—Report of the Committee for Stage 1 of the Review of Migrant and Multicultural Programs and Services,* Canberra, AGPS, 1986.

5. *An Issue of Social Justice—Review of the Ethnic Affairs Commission of Victoria,* Melbourne, Victorian Government, 1986.

6. See Speech by the Hon. R.J.L. Hawke, Melbourne, 13 March 1987.

7. Jerzy Zubrzyki, claims to have first used the term in print in his paper for the National Citizenship Convention of 1968.

8. Compare D.L. Jayasuriya, "Ethnic Minorities and Issues of Social Justice in Contemporary Australian Society," Address to Australian Adult Education Conference, Canberra December 1986.

9. This issue was discussed by Jerzy Zubrzycki in his paper for the AIMA National Research Conference in May 1986.

10. Jean Martin, *The Migrant Presence.* Sydney, George Allen and Unwin, 1978, and *The Ethnic Dimension,* Sydney, George Allen and Unwin, 1981.

11. Compare Jayasuriya, loc. cit.

12. This has been a major focus of the work of the Research and Policy Division of the Victorian Ethnic Affairs Commission, and has been embodied in numerous working papers. See also: G. Bottomley and M. de Lepervanche, *Ethnicity, Class and Gender in Australia.* Sydney, George Allen and Unwin, 1984.

13. This approach was first developed in detail by Paolo Totaro in *Participation,* NSW Ethnic Affairs Commission 1978, and then in *Access and Equity,* Victorian Ethnic Affairs Commission, 1983.

14. Jayasuriya, loc. cit.

15. See, for instance, A. Jakubowicz in: Bottomley and de Lepervanche, loc. cit.

16. I have argued elsewhere that international labor migration should not be seen as a single act, but as a process which may take several generations. The first phase is normally that of labor migration of young adults. This is followed by a phase of family reunification. The third phase is that of settlement and community formation; in situations of structural racism the third phase often involves marginalisation and definition as ethnic minorities. This concept is developed for Western Europe in: S. Castles et al., *Here for Good—Western Europe's New Ethnic Minorities* London, Pluto Press, 1984.

17. See the two reports of AIMA, *Ageing in a Multicultural Society,* Melbourne, 1985; and *Community and Institutional Care for Aged Migrants in Australia—Research Findings,* Melbourne, 1986.

18. See AIMA, *Reducing the Risk—Unemployed Migrant Youth and Labour Market Programs,* Melbourne 1985.

19. Jayasuriya, op. cit.

20. The Centre of Multicultural Studies is planning a study on self-employment of migrants in Sydney, to examine the significance of changing stratification patterns, and their relation to shifts in economic structure.

21. Des Storer, *Migrant Worker Unemployment in Victoria: Trends and Policy Directions,* Melbourne, Victorian Ethnic Affairs Commission, 1985.

22. N. Norman and K. Meikle, *The Economic Effects of Immigration on Australia.* Melbourne, Council for the Economic Development of Australia, 1985; Speech to the CEDA Forum by Chris Hurford, 11 June, 1986.

23. It is important to distinguish between the New Right approach to immigration and multiculturalism (i.e. in favor of the former, but against the latter), and the Blainey- style populism, echoed by Ruxton, which opposes both.

24. *ACTU Submission on the Immigration Program Intake 1987-8,* Melbourne, 1987.

25. The most comprehensive exposition of this approach is: BMLR *Migrant's in the Australian Labour Market,* Canberra, AGPS, 1986, which summarises a number of research papers of the BMLR and the CEPR.

26. See Jakubowicz and Castles, loc. cit. for sources and a discussion of this approach.

27. B. Bullivant, loc. cit., R. Birrell, A. Seitz, *The Ethnic Problem in Education: The Emergence and Definition of an Issue,* Melbourne, Paper for the AIMA Re-

search Conference, 1986.

28. BMLR, loc. cit., p. 155.

29. A look at the Agenda and List of Participants of the Conference on the Economic Impact of Immigration, organised jointly by the DIEA and the ANU Centre for Economic Policy Research in April 1987, shows how much this paradigm has become a guide to Government policy.

30. This argument is discussed in S. Castles, M. Kalantzis, B. Cope, "W(h)ither Multiculturalism?" loc. cit.

31. Jayasuriya loc. cit.

32. See *An Issue of Social Justice,* loc. cit., pp.30-31 and passim.

33. Netherlands Scientific Council for Government Policy, *Ethnic Minorities,* The Hague, 1979.

# The Bicentenary and the Failure of Australian Nationalism
## with Bill Cope, Mary Kalantzis, and Michael Morrissey.

By international and historical standards, Australia is a very quiet place. Despite this appearance, things of world-historical significance have happened here. Few conquests have been so systematic and brutal as that of Aboriginal society. Here our quiet is deceptively a product of the very severity of the conquest and consequently, an active silencing of historical guilt and possible arguments about reparations. The other event of world historical importance is Australia's post-war immigration. Again, the quiet of this place deceives. It has been a program of incomparable size internationally in the past half-century: a first world society with low birth rates has doubled its population, to a significant extent through immigration, in forty years. No other nation state has been as actively involved in the recruitment of immigrants. Nowhere have the sources of immigrants been so diverse.

### Defining Australia

Settler colonialism and mass immigration gave a special flavor to attempts to construct an ideology of the Australian nation. According to Benedict Anderson, 1987 was the 200th anniversary of the birth of the nation state. The "extraordinary invention" which was to become an "unproblematic planetary norm" came to the world, says Anderson, in the shape of the Constitution of the United States of America.[1]  The nation whose 200th anniversary we are called upon to celebrate in 1988 was founded just one year later. That would make it the first completely modern nation.

This view of Australia may put quite a strain on our credulity: did the convicts know they were coming to found a nation? Did they want to? Do the descendants of the Aborigines who saw the First Fleet land see things that way? Was a nation founded at all? After all, our monarch still lives overseas; many of our basic institutions are imported from our former Imperial ruler. If so, when was it founded? In 1788, in 1901 at the time of Federation, with the Statute of Westminster in 1928 or when appeals to the Privy Council were abolished in the mid-1980s? But what is a nation anyway, in a world in which crucial economic and political decisions are no longer made at the national level, especially for the smaller states?

Originally published as "The Bicentenary and the failure of Australian Nationalism." Centre for Multicultural Studies, Occasional Papers Series no. 5. (November 1987) University of Wollongong, Australia. Reprinted with permission.

It is necessary to grapple with some of the more significant recent attempts at making nationhood. In particular, we want to look at the effort to define the Australian nation as "multicultural," which began in the early 1970s, and continues, despite some controversy, to enjoy the support of all major political forces.

Multiculturalism is an ideology which calls for a celebration of cultural diversity, as an ongoing feature of Australian society?[2] It thus appears as a departure from previously prevailing racist and nationalistic stereotypes of the nation. But this progressive move bears problems: how is the tension between ethnic pluralism and the cohesiveness of society as a whole to be resolved? How can a nation be defined, if not in terms of ethnic identity: shared history, traditions, culture and language? How are core values and acceptable behavioral forms to be laid down, if the dominance of Anglo- American culture is no longer accepted? The problems of a multi-ethnic state are neither new nor unique in the world, but the response of multiculturalism is certainly a new departure in the history of Australia. So we must ask what multiculturalism means, and if it is a viable way of defining the nation.

But we must also ask if it is to be taken at face value. Has it really changed the ethnocentric structures which are so entrenched in every area of Australian life? Is it even meant to? It is also seen by some as a form of social control, a way of incorporating ethnic middle classes into the Australian political system, and using them to control their less successful compatriots, at a low cost to the state.[3]

The year 200 is a good moment to discuss attempts to define the nation, for the most obvious of these attempts is the Bicentenary itself. The Bicentennial Authority has been working for nearly a decade to:

> . . .plan, co-ordinate and promote a year long programme of local, national and international activities and events to celebrate Australia's Bicentenary and to involve 16 million Australians in the celebrations and events of 1988.[4]

As a planned, state-run exercise in the creation of a national idea, the Bicentenary is almost without precedent: for a whole year we are called upon to "join in the activities of 1988 and to celebrate what it means to be Australian".[5]

The Bicentenary is to be multicultural. We are told "Australians will really be "Living Together" in 1988". The Bicentennial Authority has developed a "set of planning objectives" to achieve this:

> To celebrate the richness of diversity of Australians, their traditions and the freedoms which they enjoy. To encourage all Australians to understand and preserve their heritage, recognize the multicultural nature of modern Australia, and look to the future with confidence. To ensure that all Australians participate in, or have access to, the activities of 1988, so that the Bicentenary will be a truly national programme in both character and geographic spread.[6]

There we have it: we must be multicultural to be national. And how shall we do it? The Authority tells us:

> Plant shrubs, hedges and trees. . .make community litter bags. . .Re-enact an episode from your district's past. . .Make a census of the headstones. .Organize an Australian Trivial Pursuit Game. . .Bake an Australia-shaped cake for a raf-

fle...Plan to have a meal from a different culture at least once a month in 1988...Paint a giant Bicentennial Living Together sign...[7]

But whatever you do, don't remind the public of unpleasant realities. In 1987, the Bicentennial Authority asked Ms. Franca Arena, a NSW State Labor MP and Justice Michael Kirby, President of the NSW Court of Appeal to write articles for its glossy journal *Bicentenary 1988*. Ms. Arena wrote of migrants' encounters with "racists, bigots and intolerant people," and called for Australia to become a republic, since the monarchy was meaningless for many Australians. Justice Kirby described the unjust, destructive and discriminatory impact of the legal system on Aboriginal culture, and drew attention to concern about the disproportionate number of Aboriginals in jail. Their articles were rejected. Our image of multicultural Australia is meant to be at the level of Trivial Pursuit: song and dance, food and folklore.

The Bicentenary itself is likely to be forgotten soon enough. It is one of history's one-night stands. But it is part of a long tradition of attempts to define Australia, and what it means to be Australian. Why is there such a need to do this? Donald Horne has pointed to the process of "reality- creation" required to establish new national states:

"There are many characteristics a new nation-state might be seen as having. Only some of them prevail. In the processes that precede the formation of new nation-states great acts of imaginative construction occur, out of which the new nation is born.[8]

There is no doubt that the creation of a national ideology is part of the political process of establishing the nation. The question of which national characteristics prevail, depends on the balance of social forces within this process. Those who have the power to create and rule a nation-state, have the most influence in defining the "national character". The definition may embody abstract ideals (liberty-equality-fraternity) and it might satisfy a popular desire to "belong," but is linked just as much to the economic and political interests of the definers.

Now, if we are to follow Anderson, we all belong to "new nations," for all modern nations are a product of the last two centuries, being closely linked to the economic and political processes of work and development.[9] Nor is the "reality creation" of the national character something that happens once, at the beginning of a new nation.[10] Rather there is a constant process of asserting, questioning, re-defining and examining the national identity. As Horne writes: The great drama, endlessly playing, is that of maintaining definitions of the nation and its social order: definitions are being repeated daily, hourly, of what the nation and society are.[11]

So Australia's definers are doing what those of all nations do, when they put forward a national image. But they seem to do so with more regularity and fervor. Richard White starts his book on "Inventing Australia" by calling it "the history of a national obsession". He points out that "Australia has long supported a whole industry of image-makers to tell us what we are".[12] White does not tell us why Australia should be a for-runner in this field. We may speculate that the cause lies in some of the ambiguities of the Australian condition. In seizing what they called empty lands, the colonists denied the humanity of their Aboriginal predecessors' very existence. For the white invaders, there was no history before 1788. This Australian nationalism had to start from a year zero, or it has to regard itself as part of the history of the "British race".[13] Australia grew as part of the British Empire. Unlike the USA, India or Britain's other far-flung possessions, Australia never managed a decent independence movement, let alone a liberation struggle. Australia was made a nation by an Act of the British parliament in 1901. The creation of a nation in a struggle for independence is usually the pre-eminent moment for the definition of national character, language, culture and myths. Australia has missed out on this, and has therefore had to make a more conscious effort to define itself. The task has not been made easier by its geographical position. On the other side of the world from its "mother country" and sitting on the edge of Asia, the maintenance of Britishness puts a strain on resourcefulness and imagination, especially as Britain's economy has faded and its Empire has crumbled.

White has documented the changing attempts to define the "Australian type": the muscular sunburnt bushman, the "Coming Man," whose self-reliance and physical prowess would renew the British race, the Digger, who proved himself at Gallipoli, the Bondi lifesaver:

> The emphasis was on masculinity, and on masculine friendships and team- work, or "mateship" in Australia. All the clich s—man of action, white man, manliness, the common man, war as a test of manhood—were not sexist for nothing. Women were excluded from the image of the "Coming Man", and so were excluded from the image of the Australian type as well.[14]

Being Australian has always been defined in sexist terms. It has also been defined in racist terms. In the early days, the pioneers' battle against the hard land was also seen as a struggle against the dangerous and wily blacks. Later the fight was against migrants who would dilute the British character of the nation, and undermine the race. The main threat was the "yellow peril" and above all the Chinese who started coming in the mid-19th century. But there was hostility towards all "non-Britishers". One of the first Acts of the new parliament in 1901 was to pass the Immigration Restriction Act, designed to keep out non-European immigrants, and popularly known as the White Australia Policy. Humphrey MacQueen has drawn attention to the role of racism in the construction of the Australian labor movement.[15] The restriction of immigration and the call for a white Australia were themes which had mobilized workers and their organization—the unions and the Australian Labor Party in the latter half of the 19th century and which would continue to do so until the Second World War.

The Immigration Restriction Act was not generally used to keep out European settlers, although they were relatively few in number until 1947. Those who did come encountered considerable hostility. Australian workers were often unwilling to work with them. In the isolationist mood of the Depression era, attempts were made to exclude non-British migrants, and to combat the influence on other cultures within Australia. At Kalgoorlie in 1934 several people were killed in "anti-dago" riots.[16] Attempts by employers to employ new migrants at low wages or to recruit them as strike breakers did not help matters.

So the Australian type was constructed in terms of the white, masculine outdoor person originating from the British Isles. Even that was contradictory enough in the light of the struggles between English and Irish. These came to a head during the First World War in the context of the Irish fight for Independence and the conflict on conscription in Australia. The concept "Anglo-Celtic", commonly used in debates on multiculturalism today, is an ill-conceived monstrosity, which can only partially paper over the gulf. One of the problems of defining the Australian nation is that its supposed sub-stratum—the British nation—does not exist either. There is indeed a British nation-state, but it uneasily embraces at least four nations (or ethnic groups).[17]

There is, however, another side to the Australian type which was being constructed before 1945. The muscular bushman/digger/life-saver was working- class. He was a "battler", who did not take kindly to authority. It was a populist image, that fitted into the concept of Australia as a "workers' paradise", where there were no aristocrats, where there was no entrenched privilege, where everyone had a chance of success. This side of the Australian type is summed up in the ideas of "mateship" and "a fair go".

How realistic was the image? From the earliest days of European settlement there was a strong measure of inequality in Australia. A landed oligarchy developed rapidly, and later merged with trading and manufacturing interests. There were class struggles throughout the 19th century, with the high demand for labor in the boom following the Gold Rush giving impetus to labor organization. The wealthier classes' demand for immigrant workers, and the existing working class' fear of dilution of labor were central political themes for much of the 19th century.[18] Contrary to ideas of the open frontier and individualism, the state played a central role in Australian development. First it was the British Imperial state, later the governments of the states and the Commonwealth, but always there was a high degree of bureaucratic control. The idea of the individualistic bushman is clearly ambiguous. On the one hand it was an attempt to assert populist values against the ruling class and the state. On the other, it was an officially propagated image, useful to conceal the reality of a highly stratified, bureaucratized and increasingly urbanized society. Crocodile Dundee has had many predecessors.

Australia's self-image, therefore, has always been problematic. It has been racist, justifying genocide and exclusionism, and denying the role of non- British migrants. It has been sexist, ignoring the role of women in national development, and justifying their subordinate position. It has idealized the role of the "common man" in a situation of growing inequality and increasingly rigid class divisions. It has been misleading, in its attempt to create a British/Australian ethnicity, while ignoring the divisions with the British nation-state, and its Australian off-shoot.

But for all that, the image might have been maintained, had it not been for Australia's post-war immigration program. The mass settlement of migrants from a wide range of countries has made the overt maintenance of racist definition of the nation and of the Australian type impossible. Today, an attempt is being made to re-interpret the immigration program as a deliberate move towards a multi-ethnic society. That is far from the truth: immigration was seen in the mid-1940s as a strategic necessity to make the country economically and militarily strong enough to repel the "yellow peril". No ethnic diversity was intended: British migrants were wanted, and when they could not be obtained in adequate numbers, the call was for "assimilable types" who would rapidly become indistinguishable from other Australians.

## Constructing Nationalism

But cultural assimilation did not take place. Australia became a country with at least 80 different ethnic groups. If the idea of a nation and of a national type is needed to secure social cohesion, then Australia is faced with a new problem: how to define these in a non-racist and non-monocultural way. According to Ernest Gellner:

> ...nationalism is a theory of political legitimacy, which requires that ethnic boundaries should not cut across political ones, and in particular, that ethnic boundaries within a given state...should not separate the powerholders from the rest.[19]

In other words, nationalism is based on the idea that every ethnic group or nation should have its own state, with all the appropriate trappings: flag, army, Olympic team and postage stamps. People relate to these symbols. A feeling of nation-ness is an integral part of their lived experience. But what happens when the people of a nation state consist of more that one ethnic group with different symbols and lived experiences? This is a common enough situation, but in the nationalist view of the world, it is likely to lead to conflict. As soon as people become conscious of their destiny as a nation they will either subjugate the other ethnic groups within the state boundaries, or, if they belong to a minority, they will fight for their own state.

Pre-industrial states, including the greatest empires, were held together not by national feeling, but by a system of power, symbolized by the divinely appointed monarch. For a colonial subject, loyalty to the British Crown had nothing to do with ethnicity. The modern nation-state, in its ideal form as a democratic republic, cannot exist on this basis. Since power belongs to the people, and is only delegated to the state (in its classical triad of legislative, executive, judicative), legitimacy cannot rest on loyalty to the state. The state is an instrument of the people; being loyal to it is a tautology. Legitimacy is based on the will of the people, and that makes it imperative to know clearly who constitutes the people: "Nationalism is primarily a political principle, which holds that the political and national unit should be congruent."[20] The struggle to make the state and the nation congruent have been at the root of much of the slaughter of our century.

In fact there are very few countries today which are ethnically homogenous. The process of industrialization and modernization leads to larger state units, embracing a variety of ethnic groups. There are few advanced countries without their "old" minorities such as the Bretons in France, the Basques and Catalans in Spain. Sometimes this often develops into serious cleavage as in Italy and in Britain. Moreover, the process of development almost always involves rural-urban migrations which quickly transcend national boundaries: in the 19th century the Irish came to Britain, the Poles to Germany, the Italians to France and Switzerland, and people from all over Europe to the USA, Canada, and some South American countries. Since 1945, there has been large-scale labor migration to most Western European countries, to North America and Australia, leading to the development of significant new ethnic minorities throughout the First World.

In encouraging labor migration, the states concerned followed short-term labor market interests, with little consideration of the long-term consequences. There was certainly no desire to create multi-ethnic societies. Now that this has happened, there are various responses: *laissé faire,* state racism or exclusionism, assimilationism, and multi-culturalism.

Whatever policy is followed, a new situation has to be dealt with: membership of the collectivity is no longer simply a result of birth: the boundary of the collectivity cannot easily be defined according to a myth of common origin or fate. If nationalism is a crucial social ideology then a new way must be found to define the nation. Nowhere is this problem more pressing than in Australia, where the post-war migrations have been so large in scale, that they have transformed the ethnic composition of the population. Forty percent of the Australian people today are immigrants or children of immigrants. Half of these are of non-British origin.

Sixty years ago, J. Lyng could write:

> The position can be compared with that of a river, started by a small spring in the mountains, winding its way through unknown country, gaining in volume and importance as it flows along, till, at the end of its course, it has become a mighty stream with incalculable potentialities. Here and there the river is made slightly bigger by tributaries.[21]

The river was "English language", "English culture" and "British stock" (an interesting juxtaposition). The tributaries were the most "modest contributions" of "non-Britishers". Even in the 1950s it was possible to assert:

> Our life is still British wholecloth, so to speak, and though the warp-threads may have turned a little, they are still strong; we have only coloured and arranged the weft-threads a little differently.[22]

With hindsight, we can say that such a view of the world was ethnocentric and mistaken even then. But it did provide a workable basis for a national ideology.

That ideology could not survive the fundamental changes resulting from the crumbling of the British Empire, the post-war immigration program and increasing vocal claims by Aboriginal groups. What were the alternatives? Other new, immigrant nations have had to contend with this problem. It is easy to understand the concepts that can hold the USA together, without recourse to ethnic identity: they include the revolutionary tradition, the force of new universalistic ideals, the strength of the "American way of life", the fascination of world power, the integrative force of modernism and innovation. Australia can only aspire to such ideals in an imitative, second-rate way. In the 1950s, attempts to define the nation focused on "the Australian way of life". The image was one of a prosperous suburban society, in which every man had his house and garden, his Holden and his hobby. Again it was a sexist image, centred around the man as bread-winner for a neat and happy nuclear family.[23]

It was a new image, that could compete with increasingly irrelevant Anglo- centric traditions. And it could draw in the New Australians: you did not have to come from Britain to want a Holden and a house, to be a good worker and trade unionist, and to support the idea of a fair go. Consumerism matched the idea of assimilationism: to be Australian meant simply to conform in terms of work and lifestyle. The ideology of "the Australian way of life" appeared as the pinnacle of modernism: pride in economic progress, technical advance and a high standard of living was to make differences in origin, race and ethnic background meaningless.

## The Rise of Multiculturism

But by the 1970s, this approach was failing, and there was a need for a new national ideology. There were several reasons for this. First, the modernist, assimilationist principle had only scratched the surface of a society still highly elitist and dominated by Anglo-centric values. Second, the onset of recession and restructuring of the world economy was making Australian living standards vulnerable. Third, trends towards economic and social segmentation linked to race, ethnicity and gender were making the whole concept of "the Australian way of life" questionable. The idea of "multiculturism" was an attempt to modify existing concepts of the nation to match up to the new realities.

Whitlam's Minister of Immigration, Al Grassby, announced his version of a "multi-cultural society of the future" in 1973. The Labor Government made efforts to take account of "migrant needs" in its social policies. From 1975, Fraser's neo-conservative government took up the slogan, and by the end of the decade had worked multiculturism up into a full-blown ideology for the Australian nation. Multiculturism has been embraced by the Hawke Labor Government, which was elected in 1983, and by the various state governments. and remains a multi-party consensus.

Australian multiculturism has two facets. The first is "ethnic politics", which began as part of a program of social democratic reform. As such it was not without its intrinsic merits. In the area of education for example, specialist English-as-a-Second-Language teaching was a genuine attempt to right the specific disadvantage suffered by children of non-English speaking background. Multicultural policy in education prescribed social reform, based on an understanding that some groups are disadvantaged. Cultural patterns, viewed by "ethnic politics" as group life-chances and wider structural relations, needed to be changed.

The second facet is the social policy of "cultural pluralism" which came to be the official embodiment of the multicultural response to ethnic politics as neo-conservatism gained sway. In some senses cultural pluralism did almost the opposite of ethnic politics. It did not set out to reform society. It merely wished to describe society as it was in order to celebrate its diversity.

For cultural pluralism the culture in multiculturalism must be those things which "already exist" in "diversity": the "interesting" and the "colorful", personal "lifestyles" and "relationships", "identifications" and "points of view". These belong to "the essentially private domain of family and religious belief".[24] This world is also the realm of "folk art . . ., dancing, music, craft and literature. . . ."[25]

In some senses, "ethnic politics" and cultural pluralism are at odds. The two views, however, often exist simultaneously in self-contradiction. On the one hand, the focus is on getting into the same cultural act as the dominant groups. On the other hand, the focus is on maintaining the diversity (which often, and perhaps conveniently, happens not to be a diversity of social equals). On the one hand, there are de-facto arguments for structural assimiliation without tears (with the cultural imperatives and ethos that accompany this). On the other hand, there is an ideology of pluralism, implacably hostile to any suggestion that assimilation might be going on. On the one hand, there is a view that migrants are "disadvantaged" and need to learn new cultural skills which open up mobility opportunities. On the other hand, the same thing is called "diversity" which is to be cherished and left alone. On the one hand, social prescription is a rationale for reform. On the other hand, social description is a celebration of what is.

But, having said this, there are also elements of consistency to be found between ethnic politics and cultural pluralism. First, cultural pluralism is a handy and inexpensive solution to the problem of ethnic politics. Second, both cultural pluralism and ethnic politics transpose, albeit by slightly different logics, debates about the plight of minorities from a realm which might in part involve critical structural analysis to an analysis simply of "culture" or "ethnicity".

The most fundamental question then, is why bother trivializing the notion of culture? Whatever the inadequacies of a theory, such as the reformist vision of ethnic politics, which tries to give all social groups tickets in the lottery of social mobility, at least it admits social disadvantage and wants to find ways of righting it. But when the multiculturalists attempt to discuss what they mean by the culture we can find in diversity, they shift from social prescription to social description, from the imperatives of reform to a celebration of what exists. At best, multiculturalism is an escape, a consolation for "the increasing alienation of the individual from the complexities and pressure of modern society. The nation is simply too large, too amorphous, too remote and impersonal to offer a satisfactory basis for wider relationships".[26] Cultural pluralism in other words can help to overcome or prevent the insecurity, homogenization and loss of personal identity characteristic of mass society. It is possible to retreat into culture narrowly defined. But there is a sense in which this is precisely the effect of that brand of ethnic politics which merely sees multiculturalism as the removal of "cultural" or attitudinal barriers from minority groups to play the core cultural game, which remains fundamentally unquestioned.

### The New Right and the Attack on Multiculturalism

Multiculturalism has been attacked recently in the media. We find both the old-style racist populism of Geoffrey Blainey (a prominent historian) and of Bruce Ruxton (President of the Victorian branch of the Returned Services League), and the more subtle racism of the so-called New Right. The focus of debate has been the increasing proportion of migrants who come to Australia from Asia.

The "New Right" recognizes and abhors the crisis of unitary national identity. It puts this down in large measure to the destructive influence of a "new class" of trendy left intellectuals and public servants. By the late 1980s, wrote David Barnett in the newsmagazine *The Bulletin,* there were thousands of government employees in the multicultural industry with a "vested interest in perpetuating separate ethnic identities". The perceptions of this "New Right" are frequently very shrewd, even if their call for "anglomorphy" (following English values and life-styles) is a rather bizarre aspiration for Indo-Chinese immigrants, in contra-distinction to the somewhat different aspiration to success in the competitive world of wage labor and commodity production. "Hard multiculturalism", in order to preserve "ethnic integrity", it is pointed out, is equally liable to assist in the reproduction of traditions and values that are often grotesquely ignorant and both racist and sexist.[27] Furthermore, as L.J.M. Cooray argues in the New Right journal *Quadrant,* multiculturalism is based on a "retrogressive conception of culture," static and seeking to retard, naively against inevitable pressures, the process of cultural interaction and evolution.[28]

Both the populists like Blainey and the intellectual "New Right" represent revived versions of a racist conception of Australian identity. At the most fundamental level, both Blainey and the "New Right" recommend an ideology of unitary identity and self-assurance about the superiority of the industrial society we live in. Partly reminiscent of the glories of English colonial ideology, both inject an element of English-ness into their characterization of this society. Both advocate assimilation as the most desirable approach to cultural difference. In articulating these views, they advocate a return to the past, in critical appraisal of the development of multiculturalism and cultural pluralism generally. These are the roots of their brand of racism.

At more superficial levels, Blainey falls into modes of discourse which are more immediately and inevitably racist. Diagnosing as he does the visible phenotypical and cultural differences of "Asian'-ness to be the significant problem of racism, both in nineteenth century Australia and today, is to accept at face value the racist interpretative framework of some of the historical and social actors. Rather, visible differences are not themselves the problem. The problem is the ideology of racism as a means of (mis)- interpreting social division. Blainey follows those social actors he considers to be significant into the misconception of a supposed reality of "race" as the problem rather than "racism" as ideology.

The "New Right", on the other hand, whilst equally convinced of the virtues and supposedly inevitable realities of assimilation, evidently think the cultural difference of "Asian'-ness less great that Blainey and thus that "Anglomorphy", for any immigrant convinced of the virtues of the free enterprise society, is a viable and desirable process. Of course, in this there are very obvious assumptions about the incompatibility and undesirability of on-going cultural difference, in which frequently racist assumptions are not so deeply submerged.

Blainey and the "New Right" are not simply temporary and unpalatable social commentators. They reiterate the official policy and the dominant popular ideology of the decades up to the mid-1970s and reflect some fundamental structural and cultural processes which still persist, despite some of the pretensions of the happy ideology of cultural pluralism of the 1980s.

## Options for Australia

The dilemma is evident: the now dominant paradigm of Australia as a multicultural society will not sustain a nationalism able to perform its traditional ideological function. Put simply, the project of imagining communality, imagining the shared mission of the nation, imagining our domestic progress as all of us move simultaneously through history, is torn apart by the paradigm of cultural difference that replaces assimilation. Apart from the material fact that we can no longer believe strongly in the reality of that progress, we now also imagine formally equal and culturally relative differences, of ethnicity, gender or "lifestyle". But the "New Right" project of advocating a revival of nationalism as a way of resolving our social and economic woes is equally problematic: Its assimilationist assumptions have failed in the past, and will continue to fail due to the demographic diversity and socio-economic segmentation of Australian society.

Equally important in causing the breakdown of Australian nationalism is the growing internationalization of the economy. The decisions which determine Australian living standards and income distribution are today made on the stock-markets of Tokyo and New York, rather than by Australian governments. International commodity design and production and improving communications in turn cause an erosion of national life-styles and cultures. These themes cannot be pursued further here.

So what possibilities are available to Australia as we enter the third century of white settlement? We see four options:

## 1. Inequality plus imagined community

This means the continued integration of the economy as part of the world market, but with the development of a strong ideological basis for national identity, leading to a general commitment to the Australian nation-state. This option, as spelt out by the "New Right" seems highly unlikely to succeed, given the problems of Australian national identity described. Attempts to create a general "we-feeling" through sport, life-style symbols or indeed through the Bicentenary have had no enduring success.

## 2. Inequality plus state repression

This is the "Latin American" model, in which social and political divisions become too sharp to be accommodated in concensus-type parliamentary politics. If the Australian economy really moves into the "Banana Republic" mode envisaged by Treasurer Keating in 1986, and no equitable way of sharing the burden can be found, so that the billionaires get richer and the number of people in poverty grows, then a peaceful solution may not be possible. Under similar pressures, formally democratic states in Latin America (Chile, Uruguay) succumbed to military dictatorships in the 1970s. This option seems possible, but not likely, for concensus politics have certainly not broken down here yet.

## 3. Inequality plus fragmentation and quiescence

In this option the breakdown of social solidarity takes the form, not of polarization, but of fragmentation. Politics becomes increasingly meaningless, as the lack of real power of parliaments can no longer be concealed. Since the decisions are made in the stock exchanges of Tokyo, London and New York, and in the international corporate bureaucracies, why bother anyway? The result is hopelessness, hedonism and retreat into the private sphere. Protest takes the form of life-styles and sub-cultural groups, and can easily be co-opted by the leisure industries. Increasing drug and alcohol addiction, fundamentalist religion, mental illness and violence are products of the real powerlessness of the social being. Politics shift from interests to values, providing a focus for "New Right" ideologies of family, individuality and competition. This seems the most likely scenario of all, for it is simply an extrapolation of existing trends.

## 4. Equality plus real community

An alternative to these less than inspiring possibilities is a society based on the best elements of national Australian tradition, the most important postulates of multiculturism, and the needs and interest of the broad majority of the population. Such a political and cultural re-orientation would transcend any idea of nationalism, nation-state or simply imagined community.

The Australian traditions which should be re-asserted are not those of colonization or war, but those of the "fair go", that is of social justice for all. The image of Australia which should be brought back is that of the "workingman's paradise", though the racist and sexist aspects of this ideal would need to be worked through and modified.

The aspects of multiculturism worth maintaining are the principles of cultural self-determination and of cosmopolitan identity. They must be linked to measures to meet the specific needs of discriminated and disadvantaged groups, policies to overcome structural marginalization and labor market segmentation, and to combat racism.

Above all, the history of white racism and genocide against the Aborigines must become a central theme of education and public debate, and an accommodation with the Aborigines must be achieved through payment of reparations, Land Rights legislation, and a treaty. Steps must be taken to improve dramatically the economic and social situation of the Aboriginal population, not through welfare measures, but through making adequate resources available to Aboriginal communities and these being placed under their own control.

Any such strategy must be based on an attempt to re-define the basis of social organization, and to move away from a political emphasis on the nation-state. Our life today is determined as much by events on the local level, as by those on the level of world politics and economics. In Britain, it has been local politics which have provided hope in the wasteland of Thatcherism. There is no contradiction between attempts to build community and bring about change at the local level, political work in the national arena, and participation in world politics. ·

The Bicentenary could have been an occasion for celebration. The opportunity was thrown away by Australian political leaders' unwillingness to face up to the real issues and problems. Once the decision was taken to ignore Aboriginal demands for real expiation, the Bicentenary became a lost cause. It changed from something with potential social meaning to a public relations exercise. Bicentennial Authority propaganda let the cat out of the bag, by calling for the inclusion of youth, women, ethnic groups, Aborigines and the handicapped in the celebrations. The conclusion was inescapable: only white Anglo middle-class men really had anything to celebrate in Australia; the inclusion of the rest was tokenism. If the Bicentenary had been concerned with helping to create an all-embracing society, it would have been based on real changes, designed to secure equality

the groups mentioned, but also to bring in others, whose marginalization makes them invisible for those in power: the unemployed, those living below the poverty line, the industrial casualties, the deprived.

The Bicentenary is yet another indication of how the concept of the nation has become ideological and exclusionary, failing to embrace most of the population. The group which wields power and benefits from it gets ever smaller. More and more of us are members of minorities. Building communality means taking the real situation in our cities, suburbs and country areas as a starting point, adopting political and economic forms which correspond with the needs and interests of the many groups who are voiceless at present, and working for change everywhere. We do not need a new ideology of nationhood. We need to transcend the nation, as an increasingly obsolete relic of early industrialism. Our aim must be community without nation.

# Notes

1.  BENEDICT ANDERSON, Narrating the Nation, in: *Times Literary Supplement.* 13 June 1986.
2.  Multiculturalism has other meanings too, which will be discussed later in this book.
3.  ANDREW JAKUBOWICZ, State and Ethnicity: Multiculturalism as Ideology, in: J. Jupp (ED), *Ethnic Politics in Australia,* Sydney: George Allen and Unwin 1984.
4.  Australian Bicentennial Authority, *Fact Sheet,* no date, no place.
5.  Australian Bicentennial Authority, *How to Make it Your Bicentenary,* no place, 1987.
6.  *How to Make it Your Bicentenary*
7.  *How to Make it Your Bicentenary*
8.  Donald Horne, *The Public Culture,* London and Sydney: Pluto Press 1986. p. 8.
9.  This theory is developed in Benedict Anderson, *Imagined Communities.* London: Verso 1983. See also: Ernest Geliner, *Nations and Nationalism,* Oxford: Basil Blackwell 1983
10. Although the idea is tempting: The French National Convention decided to restart history by declaring the year of the abolition of the monarchy as year one of a new calendar, as Anderson points out: *Narrating the Nation...*
11. Horne, p.21
12. Richard White, *Inventing Australia,* Sydney: George Allen and Unwin 1981,p.viii.
13. "...it may be said to all intents and purposes, the history of the British in this country is the history of Australia". J. Lyng, *Non-Britishers is Australia,* Melbourne: University Press 1935, p.1.
14. White, *Inventing Australia,* p.83
15. Humphrey MacQueen, *A New Britannia,* Penguin 1970 16.White, p.146.
17. See Tom Nairn, *The Break-up of Britain.* London: Verso 1981
18. Marie de Lepervanche, "Australian Immigrants 1788-1940," in: E.L. Wheelwright and K. Buckley, *Essays in the Political Economy of Australian Capitalism,* Vol.1, Sydney: Australia and New Zealand Book Company 1975
19. Gellner, *Nations and Nationalism,* p.1
20. Gellner, p.1
21. J. Lyng, *Non-Britishers in Australia,* p.1
22. W.E.H. Stanner, The Australian Way of Life, in: W.V. Aughterson (ed) *Taking Stock,* Melbourne: Cheshire 1953,p.8.
23. White, Ch. 10
24. Australian Council on Population and Ethnic Affairs, *Multiculturalism for all Australians: Our Developing Nationhood,* Canberra, 1982, p.16
25. Australian Ethnic Affairs Council, *Australia as a Multicultural Society,* Canberra, 1977, p.6
26. P.W. Matthews, "Multiculturalism and Education" in *Education News,* Vol.16, No

10, 1970,p.16
27. David Barnett, "Dividing Australia: How Government Money for Ethnics is Changing our Nation," in *The Bulletin*, 18 February 1986.
28. L.J.M. Cooray, "Multiculturalism in Australia: Who Needs It?", *Quadrant*, April 1986, pp.27-29

# Global Workforce, Global Economy, Global Culture? Migration and Modernization

Mass labor migration is part of the process of industrialization and modernization. It has been significant ever since European colonial expansion heralded the development of the capitalist world economy in the 16th century. As pre-capitalist socio-economic formations were integrated into the world market, they came to participate in international flows of capital, raw materials, manufactured goods and labor, making possible "accumulation on a world scale", as Samir Amin has put it.[1] The development of multinational workforces is an integral part of the development of the world economy. Today this applies in a dual sense: workforces become multinational within each country due to migration; they become multinational on the global level as transnational corporations dot their worksites around the world.

Since 1945, the states of the developed countries have frequently attempted to regulate migration and settlement. Such efforts have not always been successful, due to the difficulties in striking a balance between the conflicting interests of different factions of capital, and of different sections of labor. Labor migration (temporary or permanent, legal or illegal) will continue as long as the capitalist world is marked by uneven development, with enormous discrepancies in income levels between different areas. As Vernon Briggs has pointed out, where wage levels vary as dramatically as on the two sides of the Mexican-United States border, no amount of policing will stop people crossing it.[2] It may be easier to stop migrants entering an island like Britain or Australia, but as communications and transport improve, and populations become more cosmopolitan, it will be harder and harder to control population movements. The great migrations of the last 150 years may be mere preludes to even more general movements and interminglings of people.

Migrations are not simply individual responses to wage differentials, as the "human capital" theorists would have us believe. They are collective actions in the context of societal and economic change. People do not move from intact, "traditional" societies, to advanced industrial countries—the stereotype of the "peasant" in the "metropolis" is misleading. Mass departures occur when capitalist penetration and the transformation of pre-capitalist societies has already begun: as the development of a money economy and competition from more advanced areas upsets existing forms of production and distribution, people lose their livelihoods, and are forced to seek entry into the modern sector of the economy. This may mean changing status (e.g. from independent peasant to agricultural wage laborer), moving to a modern city in the same country (e.g. from Anatolia to Ankara), or migrating to an industrial country (e.g. from Turkey to West Germany). One reason why migratory flows are so rarely reversed is that most people have nothing to go back to: the changes in the economy and social structure of the region of origin which caused emigration also preclude return. In addition the migrants themselves change through the experience of migration: it is hard to go back to an isolated village after life in a great city.

Migration is not an act—a single event, such as crossing a border. It is a process, which involves various stages, and which may take a lifetime—or more! The three basic stages of the migratory process are described above in Chapter 6: first migration of young, economically active persons (generally with a predominance of males); second family reunification in the new country; and third permanent settlement and—under certain circumstances—formation of ethnic minorities.[3] But these three stages are embedded in a more fundamental and longer-lasting process, which is illustrated in Figure 1.

Figure 1: Migratory Process as Part of Global Development

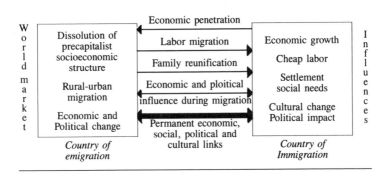

The process starts with capitalist penetration and changes in the region of origin, and leads on through labor migration, family reunification and settlement to social, cultural and political transformation of the country of immigration. The culmination of the process is the development of permanent and multifaceted links between the country of emigration and the country of immigration. This, of course, takes place in the context of the growing internationalization of economic, political and social relations ("world market influences" in the diagram). So the two countries shown for illustration are merely part of a complex network.

The point is that the postwar migrations have been one part of a historical process which has profoundly changed not only economic structure, but also the character of the nation state. Some sections of the indigenous populations of the countries of immigration find it hard to come to terms with this reality. That is why there is so much debate on policies towards immigration and the new minorities. The right-wing discourse has at its poles the alternatives of exclusion and assimilation; the liberal/left discourse oscillates between protection of national labor and multiculturalism. Nobody feels comfortable with these alternatives: all have high political costs. I will return to this below.

But first let us look briefly at the trends of the late 1980s. We need to examine both new migratory currents, and the patterns of ethnic relations emerging from the previous waves of migrations. We cannot distinguish rigidly between the two: the new migrants of the 1980s enter volatile situations of class formation and political conflict in which the economic, cultural and political rights of the new minorities are being fought out. Their entry affects the outcome of these struggles: policies on migration, settlement, citizenship and social justice have become inseparable. We will look in turn at some of the main regions affected by international migration.

We can note one common feature right away: the transnational corporations increasingly initiate and organize movements of managers, specialists and consultants within their own global networks. Such movements are mostly of a temporary nature, and concern highly-qualified personnel. Nation states have little control over these movements, though they generally favor them. The experts move between advanced industrial countries, oil-producing countries, newly industrializing countries (NICs), and underdeveloped countries. Migrations of personnel in the frameworks of the international governmental organizations (e.g. UNO, IMF, OECD) are similar in character.

## Western Europe

As outlined in several of the articles in this book, the major period of labor migration to most Western European countries was 1945 to 1973, especially the latter part of that period. Family reunification was large in volume in the 1970s. Britain is an exception: primary migration was virtually stopped in 1962, and family reunification mainly took place in the 1960s and early 1970s. Net immigration (the balance between immigration and emigration has been low for most countries in the 1980s. Indeed, more people have left than have arrived in some years.

Mass labor migration has not resumed and is not expected to, in view of persistent unemployment. However, there is some talk of a renewed need for labor in the near future, when the depleted birth cohorts of the 1960s reach working age, especially in the Federal Republic of Germany (FRG). But labor recruitment from outside the European Community is not generally regarded as politically acceptable. Movements within the European Community (and within the Nordic Labor Market which embraces the Scandinavian countries) continue. They mainly involve highly-skilled persons, moving temporarily, and are different in character from the mass migrations of the pre-1973 period. Some relatively low-skilled workers (such as building workers) do still migrate within the Community—especially from Italy and Ireland. At the same time, some countries are now experiencing both emigration and immigration: Italy, Greece and Spain all have influxes of workers from Africa and Asia countries. These streams are largely unregulated, and most migrants work without documents. One stream of entrants that continues and is even growing is that of Third World refugees. Their motivation for migration is not economic, nor do they intend to settle, but they do tend to get the low-status jobs typical of migrant workers. Moreover the impact of xenophobic campaigns against refugees has done much to stimulate racism against all migrants.

So the main issue in Western Europe is not immigration, but rather the societal position of the new ethnic minorities, which have developed out of the postwar migrations. Table 1 gives information on the number of foreign residents in some Western European countries. The

Appendix Table 1: Foreign Population in Western European Countries (thousands)

| Coutry of Origin | Belgium 1983 | France 1982 | Germany 1985 | Netherlands 1985 | Sweden 1985 | Switzerland 1985 |
|---|---|---|---|---|---|---|
| Austria | .. | .. | 172.5 | 2.9 | 2.9 | 29.2 |
| Finland | .. | .. | 9.9 | .. | 138.6 | 1.4 |
| Greece | 21.1 | .. | 280.6 | 3.7 | 9.4 | 8.7 |
| Itlay | 270.5 | 333.7 | 531.4 | 17.9 | 4.0 | 392.5 |
| Portugal | 10.4 | 764.9 | 77.0 | 7.5 | 1.5 | 30.8 |
| Spain | 56.0 | 321.4 | 152.8 | 19.1 | 2.9 | 108.4 |
| Turkey | 70.0 | 123.5 | 1401.9 | 157.7 | 21.5 | 50.9 |
| Yugoslavia | 5.6 | 64.4 | 591.0 | 11.7 | 38.4 | 69.5 |
| Algeria | 10.8 | 795.9 | 5.3 | .. | 0.5 | 1.9 |
| Morocco | 119.1 | 431.1 | 48.1 | 117.3 | 1.1 | 1.4 |
| Tunisia | 6.8 | 189.4 | 23.1 | 2.6 | 0.7 | 2.1 |
| Other Countries | 320.6 | 655.8 | 1085.3 | 212.0 | 167.1 | 242.9 |
| TOTAL | 890.9 | 3680.1 | 4378.9 | 552.4 | 388.6 | 939.7 |
| As % of total population | 9.0 | 6.8 | 7.2 | .. | 4.6 | 14.6 |

*Source:* OECD Continuous Reporting System on Migration (SOPEMI) 1986, Paris, OECD, 1986

total number is around 11 million. Britain is not included in the table, but at the time of the 1981 Census had 3.4 million overseas-born persons, of whom 1.5 million were from the New Commonwealth (mainly the Caribbean and the Indian sub-Continent), and about 600,000 from the Ireland. The figures are only approximations and there are problems of comparability, but they do give an idea of the size of the the immigrant populations. To these 14 million must be added those children of immigrants born in Western Europe who have the citizenship of the country of immigration (not all do). For instance there are over 1 million naturalized persons in France. Half the black people in Britain were born in the country. Just to get a rough idea, we can say that there are at least 16 million people of migrant origin in western Europe, making up between 5 and 15 per cent of the populations of various countries. Britain, France and the German Federal Republic all have over 4 million people of immigrant origin, of whom 40-50 per cent are of non-European origin.[4]

Chapter 6 above pointed to some of the consequences of the end of the guest-worker system for Western European society and Chapters 4 and 5 pointed to some of the effects in specific areas—labor relations and education in the FRG. In brief, most migrants and their children remain—if employed—manual workers in manufacturing, construction and the services. There has been some social mobility, but not enough to change the basic fact that labor markets remain highly segmented by ethnicity and gender. The segmentation is maintained by various forms of discrimination ranging from preference for nationals (laid down by law), to informal racism. However, migrant workers have borne the main brunt of restructuring, and everywhere have above average rates of unemployment; many have withdrawn from the formal workforce altogether.

A process of social segregation is also evident: many migrants are highly concentrated in inner-city areas, where housing and social facilities are often deficient. It is in such districts that competition with the worst-off groups of the indigenous populations becomes evident, leading to racism and conflict. In this situation, the "foreigner problem" or the "immigrant issue" has become a main theme of political discourse. Anti-foreigner or anti-black campaigns have been at the center of the resurgence of the extreme right in most Western European countries. Mainstream politicians of the center-right have increasingly taken up such themes, calling for policies of repatriation, restriction of minority rights, and denial of citizenship rights. The power of such slogans became evident in the mid-1980s, with the electoral success of the Front National in France.

But the clock cannot be turned back. As immigrant communities consolidate themselves in a situation of restricted rights and economic crisis, they develop their own institutional structures and informal labor markets. It seems likely that much movement between emigration and immigration countries escapes official notice, even in countries like the FRG, where controls are rigorous. Many individuals and families see themselves as belonging to two societies, and find social and economic niches in both. In the multinational areas of the big cities, ethnic minority small business brings a new (though often unacknowledged) economic dynamism, which helps to arrest processes of urban decline. The development of economic and social infrastructures helps make the maintenance of minority languages and culture possible. Migrants are not assimilating; rather they are learning social competence in the economic and cultural practices of European industrial societies, while at the same time influencing them profoundly.

There are many people in Europe who find this process positive and stimulating. There are many more who feel threatened and bewildered. After a century of wars based (at least ostensibly) on the need to assert national interests and character, Europeans find it hard to accept that their societies are now being transformed from within. Germany is the extreme example: just 40 years after a Holocaust designed to rid the country of its historical minorities, the population finds itself confronted with new ethnic groups. The political leadership, whether of the left or of the right, has failed significantly in understanding the situation and mapping out the consequences. By asserting parrot-like that "the Federal Republic is not a country of immigration" (despite over 4 million immigrants), they block the way to political solutions. In Britain, the trauma of lost Empire and economic and political decline hamper the development of a pluralist non-racist society. In France, a failure to come to grips with historical realities, such as the Vichy Regime and the Algerian War has opened the way for a racist discourse, which puts the blame for all social problems on North African immigrants .

## The USA

Immigration has played a major role in the history of North America since the first settlements. (The following account will concentrate on the USA, although similar trends toward increased immigration and ethnic diversity may be observed in Canada). The overwhelming majority of the early settlers were Northern European Protestants, so that there was a high degree of ethnic and religious homogeneity among the citizenry at the time of Independence.[5] However the exploitation of migrant workers, which was to give rise to racial and ethnic pluralism and conflict, goes back to the 16th century in the shape of the "peculiar institution" of slavery. The industrial take-off after the Civil War was fueled by mass immigration from all parts of Europe. At the same time draconian measures were used to keep the now-emancipated Blacks in the South to provide labor power for the plantations, for cheap cotton and other agricultural products were central to the success of industrialization.

The ethnic composition of the US population was drastically changed by the nearly 30 million immigrants who entered the USA between 1861 and 1920. The largest groups were the Irish, the Italians and Jews from Eastern Europe, but all European nationalities were represented. By 1920 the Census showed that 13.9 million people had been born overseas, making up 13.2 per cent of the total population.[6] When the restrictive Immigration Act of 1921 dried up the supply of migrant labor from overseas, the factories of the Middle West, the North-East and California mobilized Black workers from the South, where the mechanization of agriculture now made them dispensable. The Great Migration of Blacks further increased the diversity and the racial/ethnic segmentation of the labor force and the population in the growing cities.

Economic crisis and a series of restrictive laws kept migration low until 1965. The 1970 Census showed that the number of overseas-born people had fallen to 9.6 million, only 4.7 per cent of the population.[7] But the Immigration Act of 1965 and subsequent amendments to it created a system of worldwide immigration, in which the most important criterion for admission was kinship with US citizens or residents. The result was a dramatic upsurge in legal immigration, with levels reaching 600,000 per year in the early 1980s. Currently, Congress is discussing further changes to the immigration system, which, if introduced, would further raise immigration levels, and put more emphasis on labor market criteria for admission.

Immigration is large in absolute terms, though it appears less significant in relation to the size of total population: about one half of a percent of total population enter each year. Nonetheless, 40 per cent of population growth in the 1970s came through immigration. By 1980 there were 13.9 million overseas-born people in the USA—6.2 per cent of total population. The largest concentrations were in New York State (13.4 per cent of total population) and California (14.8 per cent).[8] In recent year, people from Latin America and Asia have come to dominate migrant intakes, leading to a gradual shift in the ethnic composition of the population. It is predicted that Hispanics and Asians will soon outnumber Blacks in many areas of the USA.

In addition, US employers, particularly in agriculture, have made efforts to recruit temporary migrant workers ever since the First World War. Organized labor has been highly critical of this, fearing that domestic workers would be displaced and wages held down. Government policies have varied: at times systems of temporary labor migration such as the Mexican Bracero Program have been introduced; in other periods, recruitment has been formally prohibited, but tacitly tolerated. Employers have apparently benefitted from the employment of millions of undocumented workers, completely deprived of legal rights.

The Immigration Reform and Control Act (IRCA) of 1986 introduced a limited amnesty for undocumented workers. Something like one and one half million people came forward by the cut-off date of May 4 1988 (the cut-off date for agricultural workers is November 30 1988). Nobody knows what proportion of illegals did not come forward for various reasons. There are thought to be several million, whose conditions will now be even worse, as employer sanctions mean that it will be extremely hard for them to find any work. At present, agricultural employers are lobbying for the admission of large numbers of "replacement agricultural workers" (as provided for by IRCA), since they fear that legalized workers will depart for better jobs. The USA appears to be on the brink of a guest-worker system, which will no doubt lead to further uncontrolled permanent settlement in the future.

The USA, like Western Europe has become more cosmopolitan in its ethnic composition through recent migrations. In retrospect this tendency appears as part of the process of "internationalization" of the US economy.[9] International trade rose from 9 per cent of gross national product in 1950 to 25 per cent in 1980. No doubt this trend has accelerated in the 1980s, as the USA has become the world's largest international debtor. Paradoxically, the "internationalization" and the relative decline of the US economy is a result of the period of US world economic hegemony which followed the Second World War.

US dominance allowed a restructuring and transnational integration of the world market, which has led to a proliferation of international links. Just as European colonialism and hegemony eventually led to the immigration of colonized peoples to the metropoles, now the peoples of the USA's neo-colonial world empire are coming to the center. This process is likely to continue. In view of the USA's historical difficulties with ethnic and racial conflicts, this probability should give policy-makers cause to plan ahead, to ensure social justice and equal opportunities for all groups. However, nothing in US traditions nor in current reactions to ethnic diversity leads us to the optimistic expectation that this will in fact come about.

**Australia**

Postwar migration has made Australia the most ethnically diverse of all highly-developed nations: about 20 per cent of the population are immigrants, and a further 20 per cent belong to the "second generation". Although people from Britain and Ireland are the largest single group, they are outnumbered by people of non-English speaking background. The immediate postwar migrants came from Northern and Eastern Europe, then from Southern Europe and the Near East, most recently from South East Asia, the Indian Sub-Continent, New Zealand and the Pacific Islands. Like the USA, Australia has stressed entry of family members of Australian residents and of refugees—in recent years about two thirds of entrants have belonged to these categories.

Chapters 7 and 8 describe the consequences of ethnic diversity for social policy and concepts of national identity in Australia. In the late 1960s and 1970s, politicians reluctantly abandoned their assimilationist ideals, and recognized the inevitability of ethnic pluralism. Changes in immigration policy—particularly the abandonment of the "White Australia Policy" were efforts to come to terms with the realities of Australia's economic and geographic situation. The policy of "multiculturalism", introduced in the late 1970s was designed as a framework to manage the social and particularly the educational issues arising from ethnic diversity. As the two Chapters show, the apparent consensus on multiculturalism conceals some fundamental disagreements on what this principle should mean in terms of structural change and social policy.

It is not necessary to repeat the arguments of the two Chapters here. Recent developments show that many questions are still open. In late 1987, the Federal Government appointed a Committee to Assess Australia's Immigration Policy (CAAIP). Its findings have not been published at the time of writing, but rumor has it that stress will be put on increasing immigration quotas, greater selectivity according to labor market criteria, and a more pronounced opening to Asia. Already, migrant intakes have been increased to over 130,000 for the coming year, and increasing stress is being put on the Business Migration Program (which gives preference to entrepreneurs who bring capital to

Australia).

The postwar migrations have made the Australian population so cosmopolitan that a return to a monocultural, anglocentric view of the world seems unthinkable. Certainly, there are groups which struggle against the trend, and advocate a resurrection of the glorious isolationism of the past, but they have been conspicuously unsuccessful in mobilizing mass support for racist or assimilationist strategies. Australia could, willy-nilly, prove to be a laboratory for a retreat from the nation state based on ethnic boundaries, which has been the norm for eurocentric societies for the last two centuries. That would be an irony of history: for an outpost of British colonialism built on genocide against the Aboriginal population to become truly internationalist in outlook would give a new twist to the dialectic of modernization. Let us not cheer too soon.

## Oil-Producing Countries

We turn now briefly to new patterns of migration which have emerged in the 1970s and 1980s: recruitment of labor for oil-producing countries, and movement of workers to newly-industrializing countries.

The dramatic increase in oil revenues after 1973 led many OPEC and other oil-producing countries to embark on ambitious programs of industrialization which went far beyond the capacities of their domestic labor forces. This led to massive recruitment of migrant workers. Kuwait, for instance had 213,000 foreign workers in 1975 and 384,000 by 1980. In the latter year they made up no less than 78 per cent of the labor force. In 1980 there were 2.7 million migrant workers in the Gulf oil states.[10] The workers came mainly from Arab countries, particularly from Palestine and Jordan, but also from other Islamic countries like Pakistan and Bangladesh, and from non-Islamic countries like the Phillipines. Libya recruited mainly in Egypt. Some of the feudal rulers of the Gulf were nervous of the possible political impact of Palestinians, and actually preferred non-Arabs. In any case, strict measures were taken to ensure that workers did not settle permanently. Family entry was prohibited and length of stay was limited. Legal and administrative frameworks were reminiscent of the West European guestworker systems of the 1960s.

Non-Arab oil countries also looked to migrant labor: Venezuela was reported to have half a million foreign workers, and to be expecting to import another half million by the late 1970s. They came from other Latin American countries, but also Spain, Portugal and Italy.[11] Large numbers of workers streamed into Nigeria from other African countries in response to the oil-boom. In both these cases there was little state control or planning. Spontaneous flows of undocumented workers seemed to match well with labor demand.

When the oil boom began to deflate in the early 1980s, some countries adopted draconian measures: there were mass expulsions from Nigeria in 1983 and 1985, and from Libya in 1985. Undocumented workers were rounded up in large numbers and forced to leave the country immediately, which caused considerable hardship. But an analysis of migration trends in Kuwait showed that although the inflow declined, an increasing proportion of immigrant workers were remaining after the completion of their initial contract. The decline in the number of migrant workers was significantly less than expected.[12]

It appears that, despite the strict regulations governing the situation of migrants in Gulf states, certain economic and social factors do lead to longer periods of residence. These include continued demand for personnel to run the new industries, employers' desire to maintain existing labor forces, and the growing employment of domestic servants. The oil-rich Arabs seem increasingly content to have the lower-status work done by an imported laboring class. This may lead to a repetition of the European guest-worker experience: that labor migration eventually leads to settlement and to social and cultural change.

### The Newly-Industrializing Countries (NICs)

One reason for the decline in labor migration to Western Europe was the development of a "new international division of labor" (NIDL), in which labor-intensive production stages were relocated to low-wage countries in the Third World. In the advanced industrial countries, there was a reduction in employment in the mass production branches, which had relied heavily on migrant labor.[13] The leading role in this trend was taken by the transnational corporations, although some large national companies also participated. Typically, the new factories were set up in "off-shore" production areas, which provided tax concessions and other special conditions for foreign investors, in Southeast Asia, Latin America and the Caribbean. The main attraction for the foreign companies was the very low wages, long hours and lack of social costs in these areas.[14]

The result was a new wave of migratory movements, both internal and international within the Third World, as workers moved to the new world market factories. The great majority of the workers have been women, as they are regarded as more suitable for the light assembly work in the new electronics plants or for sewing garments. Employers can also take advantage of patriarchal structures, which make women workers cheaper and easier to control.

After nearly two decades of this development it is becoming evident that the NIDL is not simply a way of perpetuating the economic dependence of the former colonies on the metropoles. In some areas, such as Brazil, Taiwan, Singapore, Korea and parts of India, industrialization is no longer of a mere dependent character, and national capital is playing an important role. There are increasing differences between the NICs and the truly impoverished nations, where little development is taking place. Indeed, in view of the changes in both the OPEC countries and the NICs over the last 15-20 years, the concept of the Third World, as a socio-economic category, is becoming increasingly questionable. We have only to look at examples such as the burgeoning industrialization of Korea and the de-industrialization of Northern England to realize that the distinction between the First and Third Worlds has outlived its usefulness.

## Migration and the New International Division of Labor

The new migrations of the 1970s and 1980s imply at least a partial reversal of the current from the periphery (the underdeveloped countries) to the center (the advanced industrial countries) of the capitalist system which became established in the post-1945 period. But it is not a simple return to earlier patterns of movement of labor from the center to the periphery (as in the colonial period). Patterns have become complex and volatile: migrations are now taking place in both directions, as well as within the center and within the periphery. This reflects the fact that the growing integration of the world economy by increasingly mobile transnational capital is undermining the distinctions between center and periphery.

It would be wrong to think that the industrialization of countries like Brazil and Korea leads to a reduction of overseas migrations. As the remarks at the beginning of this chapter imply, the development of a capitalist economy devastates pre-capitalist forms of production and distribution, forcing thousands or millions of people to seek new livelihoods. Many move into the new industries in the growing cities, but for many the exploding cities of Asia and Latin America are mere staging posts on the way to Western Europe, North America or Australia. As Saskia Sassen-Koob has shown, one aspect of the NIDL is the development of global cities: centers of corporate control, design, administration and marketing, which pull in highly-qualified personnel from all over the world. These cities also attract large numbers of low-skilled migrants, to service the needs of the new international corporate elite.[15]

The result seems to be a polarization in the labor markets of the advanced industrial countries. As manufacturing employment declines, the large blue-collar working class is being squeezed from both sides. While demand for highly-trained specialists increases, there are also growing numbers of low-skilled jobs in unregulated and non-unionized branches, such as catering, the retail trades and light manufacturing. The relatively favorable and protected wages and employment conditions achieved by generations of blue-collar trade unionism are being eroded. New entrants into the labor market, particularly migrants, youth and women, find they have to enter low-skilled, non-unionized jobs, often in the informal sector, where they have little bargaining power or security of employment. Typical employment in this area is found in ethnic restaurants, fast-food chains, retail establishments, garment outwork, and sub-contracting in the construction industry. The great growth in employment of recent years, particularly in the USA and Australia, has been bought at a high price.

The internationalization of the workforce is an integral part of this development. Migrant workers (including US blacks), who became concentrated in the manual manufacturing occupations between 1945 and the mid-1970s have borne the brunt of displacement and unemployment. The new migrants of the 1970s and 1980s have been channelled into the unregulated sectors. The survival of the garment industry in Western Europe, the USA and Australia is due to the exploitation of migrant women, whose wages have been forced down almost as low as those of their counterparts in Asia and Latin America.[16] The services and public utilities of the great financial centers like New York and Los Angeles are run by Black, Hispanic and Asian workers.

The development of a global economy increases the options for capital, and makes it increasingly difficult for workers to demand a share in the control of production and distribution. But the global economy has also led to something that was neither anticipated nor planned: the development of a cosmopolitan workforce, which is to be found in every country that has been pulled into the world market. The power of the transnational corporations has already made apparent the unviability of the nation-state as an economic unit. The existence of the global workforce, which leads to ethnic diversity in all advanced countries, similarly undermines the monocultural principle upon which national identity is supposed to be constructed. If the nation state loses both its economic and its cultural basis, can its function as the essential political unit of our civilization survive? That is the question which will face us at the turn of the century.

## Notes

1. Amir, S. *Accumulation on a World Scale,* New York and London, Monthly Review Press, 1974.
2. Briggs, V.M. Jr, *Immigration Policy and the American Labor Force,* Baltimore and London, John Hopkins University Press, 1984.
3. See also Castles, S. et al, *Here for Good—Western Europe's New Ethnic Minorities,* London, Pluto Press, 1984, pp. 11-15.
4. See Castles et al. Chapter 3 for more detail.
5. Steinberg, S., *The Ethnic Myth,* Boston, Beacon Press, 1981, p. 8.
6. Briggs, p. 74.
7. Briggs, p. 74.
8. Briggs, p. 77.
9. Briggs, p. 256
10. Birks, J.S., et al., Migrant workers in the Arab Gulf: the impact of declining oil revenues, in: *International Migration Review,* vol. 20, no. 4, 1986.
11. Cohen, R. *The New Helots: Migrants in the International Division of Labor,* Aldershot, Avebury, 1987, p. 247.
12. Birk et al.
13. Fr bel, F. et al., *The New International Division of Labor,* Cambridge University Press, 1980.
14. See Cohen, pp. 242-246.
15. Sassen-Koob, S., Capital Mobility and Labor Migration: Their Expression in Core Cities, in: M. Cross (ed), *Racial Minorities and Industrial Change,* Cambridge University Press, 1987.
16. See Waldinger, R. *Through the Eye of the Needle: Immigrants and Enterprise in New York's Garment Trades,* New York University Press, 1986.

# Bibliography

1969. "L'insertion sociale des étrangers dans l'aire métropolitaine Lyon-Saint-Étienne." *Hommes et Migrations*, No.113.

1970. "Statistiques du Ministère de l'Intérieur", *Hommes et Migrations: Documents*, No. 788.

1971 *Le VIe plan et les travailleurs étrangers*, Paris.

AIMA. 1985. *Ageing in a Multicultural Society*, Melbourne.

_____ . 1986. *Community and Institutional Care for Aged Migrants in Australia—Research Findings*, Melbourne.

_____ . 1985. *Reducing the Risk—Unemployed Migrant Youth and Labour Market Programs*, Melbourne.

ACTU. 1987. *Submission on the Immigration Program Intake 1987-8*, Melbourne.

Abrams, Mark. 1969. study on prejudice in Rose, et al. *Colour and Citizenship*, pp. 551-604.

Anderson, Benedict. 1983. *Imagined Communities*. London: Verso.

_____ . 1986. "Narrating the Nation." *Times Literary Supplement*. 13 June.

*Annuaire Statistique de la France 1968.*

*Ausländische Arbeitnehmer 1969*, Nürnberg: 1970.

*Ausländische Arbeitnehmer 1970*, Nürnberg: 1971.

Australian Bicentennial Authority. 1987. *How to Make it Your Bicentenary.* no place.

Australian Bicentennial Authority. *Fact Sheet.* no date, no place.

Australian Council on Population and Ethnic Affairs. 1982. *Multiculturalism for all Australians: Our Developing Nationhood*. Canberra.

Australian Ethnic Affairs Council. 1977. *Australia as a Multicultural Society.* Canberra.

BMLR. 1986. *Migrant's in the Australian Labour Market*, Canberra, AGPS.

Bagley, Christopher. 1970. *Social Structure and Prejudice in five English Boroughs.* London.

Barnett, David. 1986. "Dividing Australia: How Government Money for Ethnics is Changing our Nation" in *The Bulletin*, 18 February.

Becker, Ruth Gerhard D¼orr, K. H. Tjaden. 1971. "Fremdarbeiterbesch¼aftigung im deutschen Kapitalismus." *Das Argument*, December.

Birrell, R. and A. Seitz. 1986. *The Ethnic Problem in Education: The Emergence and Definition of an Issue*, Melbourne, Paper for the AIMA Research Conference, 1986.

Bottomley G. and M. de Lepervanche. 1984. *Ethnicity, Class and Gender in Australia*. Sydney, George Allen and Unwin.

B. Bullivant. 1986. *Are Anglo-Australian Students becoming the New Self-Deprived in Comparison with Ethnics?* Melbourne, Monash University.

Castles, Stephen. 1980. "The Social Time-bomb: Education of an Underclass in West Germany." *Race and Class*. 21.4.

_____ . 1985. "The Guests Who Stayed—The Debate on 'Foreigners Policy' in the German Federal Republic. *International Migration Review*, 19(3), 517-534.

_____ . 1986. "The Guest-Worker in Western Europe: An Obituary." *International Migration Review.* 20.4.

_____ . 1970. "Bidonville-A French Word for Hell." *Manchester Guardian Weekley* 24.1 January.

_____ . with H. Booth and T. Wallace. 1984. *Here for Good—Western Europe's New Ethnic Minorities*, London: Pluto Press.

_____ , Bill Cope, Mary Kalantzis, and Michael Morrissey. November 1987. "The Bicentenary and the failure of Australian Nationalism." *Centre for Multicultural Studies, Occasional Papers Series no. 5.* University of Wollongong, Australia.

_____ , M. Kalantzis and B. Cope. 1986. "W(h)ither multiculturalism?" in: *Australian Society*, October 1986.

_____ and Godula Kosack. 1973, 1985. *Immigrant Workers and Class Structure in Western Europe*. London: Oxford University Press for the Institute for Race Relations.

_____. and Wiebke Wustenberg. 1979. *The Education of the Future*. London.

Center for Contemporary Cultural Studies. 1982. *The Empire Strikes Back—Race and Racism in 70s Britain*. London: Hutchinson.

Cooray, L.J.M. 1986. "Multiculturalism in Australia: Who Needs It?" *Quadrant*, April: 27-29.

Cox, Oliver Cromwell. 1970. *Caste, Class and Race*. New York.

D.G.B. 1971. "Die deutschen Gewerkschaften und die ausländischen Arbeitnehmer." Frankfurt, November 21.

DIEA. 1986. *Don't Settle for Less—Report of the Committee for Stage 1 of the Review of Migrant and Multlcultural Programs and Services*, Canberra, AGPS.

Daniels, W.W. 1968. *Racial Discrimination in England*. based on the PEP Report, Harmondsworth.

Dobler, F. 1968. "Der Streik in der hessischen Gummiindustrie im November 1967 uter besonderer Berucksichtigung der 'Dunlop' Hanaux." Hanau.

Engels, Friederich. 1962. "The Condition of the Working Class in England", in Marx and Engels. *On Britain*. Moscow.

_____. "The English Election", in *On Britain*.

*An Issue of Social Justice—Review of the Ethnic Affairs Commission of Victoria*, Melbourne, Victorian Government, 1986.

Forchungserbund. 1979. "Probleme der Ausländerbeschaftigung." *Intergierter Endbericht.*

Gavi, P. 1970. *Les Ouvriers*, Paris.

Geliner, Ernest. 1983. *Nations and Nationalism*. Oxford: Basil Blackwell.

Gienanth, Ulrich Freiherr von. 1966. in *Der Arbeitgeber*, Vol. 18.20 (March) 153.

Glyn, A. and J. Harrison. 1980. *The British Economic Disaster*. London: Pluto Press.

Grahl, J. 1983. "Restructuring in West European Industry." *Capital and Class*. 19.

Great Britain, General Register Office. 1969. *Census 1966: United Kingdom. General and Parliamentary Constituency Tables*, London: HMSO, 1969.

Hawke, R.J.L. 1987. Speech delivered in Melbourne, 13 March 1987.

Hepple, Bob. 1969. *Race, Jobs and the Law in Britain*, London: Penguin.

Horne, Donald. 1986. *The Public Culture*, London and Sydney: Pluto Press.

Hurford, Chris. Speech to the CEDA Forum, 11 June, 1986.

I.G. Metall. 1966. *Die Ausländerwelle und Die Gewerkschaften*. Frankfurt.

I.G. Metall. 1970. *Beratungsbericht zu Den Fragen Gewerkschaft und Ausländische Arbeitnehmer.* Frankfurt (February 5).

I.G. Metall. 1972. *Ergebnisse Der Betriebsratswahlen.*

I.G. Metall. 1973. *Schnell information Uber Das Ergebnis Der Vertrauensleutewahlen 1973.*

Institut für angewandte Sozialwissenschaft. 1964. *Arbelter-Vertrauensleute-Gewerkschaft.* Bad Godesberg.

_____. 1966. *Deutsche und Gastarbeiter.* Bad Godesber.

Jakubowicz, Andrew, 1984. "State and Ethnicity: Multiculturalism as Ideology." in: J. Jupp, ed. *Ethnic Politics in Australia*. Sydney: George Allen and Unwin.

_____ and S. Castles. 1987. "The Inherent Subjectivity of the Apparently Objective in Research on Ethnicity and Class," in: *Journal of Intercultural Studies*, 1.

D.L. Jayasuriya. 1986. "Ethnic Minorities and Issues of Social Justice in Contemporary Australian Society," Address to Australian Adult Education Conference, Canberra December.

Jones, K. and A.D. Smith. 1970. *The Economic Impact of Commonwealth Immigration*, Cambridge.

Kindleberger, C.P. 1967. *Europe's Postwar Growth: The Role of Labour Supply*. Cambridge, Mass.: Harvard University Press.

*Le Vle plan et les travailleurs étrangers*, Paris 1971.

Lenin. 1966. *Imperialism—the highest State of Capitalism*. Moscow.

Lyng, J. 1935. *Non-Britishers is Australia*. Melbourne: University Press.

MacQueen, Humphrey. 1970. *A New Britannia*. London: Penguin.

*Magnet Bundesrepublik*. 1966. Bonn: Informationstagung der Bundesvereinigung Deutscher Arbeitgeberverbände.

Marie de Lepervanche. 1975. "Australian Immigrants 1788-1940." in: E.L. Wheelwright and K. Buckley, *Essays in the Political Economy of Australian Capitalism*, Vol.1. Sydney: Australia and New Zealand Book Company.

119

Jean Martin. 1978. *The Migrant Presence*. Sydney, George Allen and Unwin.
————. 1981. *The Ethnic Dimension*. Sydney: George Allen and Unwin.
Marx, Karl. 1961. *Capital*, Vol. I. Moscow.
Matthews, P.W. 1970. "Multiculturalism and Education" in *Education News*. 16.10
Mitter, S. 1986. "Industrial Restructuring and Manufacturing Homework: Immigrant Women in the UK Clothing Industry," *Capital and Class*. 27.
Muller-Jentsch, Walter. 1973. "Entwicklungen und Widerspruche in der westdeutschen Gewerkschaftsbewegung," in *Gewerkschaften und Klassenkamps, Kritishes Jahrbuch '73*. Frankfurt.
Nairn, Tom. 1981. *The Break-up of Britain*. London: Verso.
Netherlands Scientific Council for Government Policy. 1979. *Ethnic Minorities*. The Hague.
Nicoladze, R.D., C. Rendu, G. Millet. 1969. "Coupable d'être malades," *Droit et Liberté*, No. 280 (March).
Norman N. and K. Meikle. 1985. *The Economic Effects of Immigration on Australia*. Melbourne, Council for the Economic Development of Australia.
OECD. 1978. *Migration Growth and Development*. Paris: OECD.
Office National d'Immigration. 1968. *Statistiques d'Immigration*. Paris.
Pfahlmann, Hans. 1968. *Fremdarbeiter und Kriegsgefangene in der deutschen Kriegswirtschaft, 1939-1945*. Darmstadt.
Phizacklea, A. 1985. "Minority Women and Restructuring: the Case of Britain, France and the Federal Republic of Germany." Paper presented at the conference on *Racial Minorities, Economic Restructuring and Urban Decline*, Center for Research in Ethnic Relations, University of Warwick.
Piehl, Ernest. 1972. "Gewerkschaften und ausländische Arbeiter," in *Gerwerkschaftsspiefel*. No. 1.
Piore, M.J. 1979. *Birds of Passage—Migrant Labor and Industrial Societies*. Cambridge.
Riehl, Rainer. 1973. "Der Aufstand der Angelernten," *Klassenkampf* (October 28).
*Review of the International Commission of Jurists*. 1969. No. 3. September.
Rose, E.J.B. et al. 1969. *Colour and Citizenship*. London.
Salowsky, Heinz. 1972. "Sozialpolitische Aspekte der Auslanderbeschaftigung." *Berichte des Deutschen Industrie instituts zur Sozialpolitik*. 6.2.
Sassen-Koob, A. 1985. "Capital Mobility and Labour Migration: Their Expression in Core Cities." Paper presented at the conference of *Racial Minorities, Economic Restructuring and Urban Decline*. Center for research in Ethnic Relations, University of Warwick.
SOPEMI. 1984. *SOPEMI-Continuous Reporting System on Migration*, Paris: OECD.
SOPEMI-Netherlands. 1985. *SOPEMI-Netherlands: Migration, Minorities and Policy in the Netherlands*, Amsterdam: Department of Human Geography, University of Amsterdam.
Stanner, W.E.H. 1953. "The Australian Way of Life." in: W.V. Aughterson (ed.) *Taking Stock*. Melbourne: Cheshire.
*Statistisches Jahrbuch der Schweiz 1967*.
Steinbeck, John. 1976. *The Grapes of Wrath*. New York: Penguin
Des Storer. 1985. *Migrant Worker Unemployment in Victoria: Trends and Policy Directions*. Melbourne, Victorian Ethnic Affairs Commission, 1985.
Thompson, E. P. 1968. *The Making of the English Working Class*. Harmondsworth.
Paolo Totaro. 1978. in *Participation*. NSW Ethnic Affairs Commission.
————. 1983. *Access and Equity*. Victorian Ethnic Affairs Commission.
United Nations Economic Commission for Europe. 1968. *Economic Survey of Europe '67*. Geneva.
Whi , Richard. 1981. *Inventing Australia*, Sydney: George Allen and Unwin.
Zubrzyki, Jerzy. 1968. paper for the National Citizenship Convention of 1968.